# THE DEVELOPMENT OF EXECUTIVE LEADERSHIP

# The Development of Executive Leadership

EDITED BY

*Marvin Bower*

PARTNER, MC KINSEY & COMPANY
CHAIRMAN, ALUMNI CONFERENCE COMMITTEE
HARVARD BUSINESS SCHOOL ASSOCIATION

HARVARD UNIVERSITY PRESS
*Cambridge, Massachusetts*
1951

PRINTED IN THE UNITED STATES OF AMERICA

SECOND PRINTING

LONDON • GEOFFREY CUMBERLEGE • OXFORD UNIVERSITY PRESS

# THE "WHY" AND "WHAT" OF THIS BOOK

A good case could be made for the proposition that the welfare and even the freedom of all Americans depends on how well we, as a nation, do in turning out an adequate number of properly equipped business leaders during the next ten years.

## IMPORTANCE OF DEVELOPING EXECUTIVE LEADERS

But there is no need to make a case for a proposition so extreme. For most thoughtful people will readily agree that the performance of business leaders during the next decade will play a major role in determining not only business but political and social trends for a long time to come. Here are some of the principal reasons:

1. *Business leaders control the economic well-being of employee and stockholder:* It is generally recognized that the single factor most responsible for the success of any free enterprise is the quality of its executive leadership. With nearly one-half of our gainfully employed persons now on the payroll of a corporation, a substantial part of our total population is directly dependent on the skill of business leaders for its economic well-being. To a lesser degree, between six and seven million stockholders and their dependents look to business leaders for all or part of their income.

2. *The course of business shapes public opinion:* Since the depression of the thirties, politicians have successfully used an unsatisfactory general level of business as a lever

for federal pump priming and business control legislation. Unless public attitudes change, any substantial and continued decline in the general level of business will be likely to produce a new crop of legislation providing for more restrictions and tighter control of business. Unfortunately, this result must now be anticipated despite the fact that the entire weight of history is against it. For history shows that restrictive legislation feeds on itself until such rigid controls must be imposed that the individuals who make up the business enterprises lose their freedom as individuals.

3. *Business leaders shape public opinion:* Since business operations have such a direct effect on social and political trends, business leaders have both a responsibility and an opportunity to use their influence to create sound public attitudes on problems not directly related to their own companies. Outstanding business leaders recognize that business responsibility now extends well beyond the plant and office door.

So, in addition to his prime responsibility of managing his enterprise at a profit, the business leader of today is faced with new and larger responsibilities. And, at the same time, the job of managing his enterprise at a profit is increasing in complexity. Consequently, the imposition of additional responsibilities makes the nation's task of developing an adequate number of properly equipped executive leaders a staggering one indeed.

## THE ATTACK ON THE TASK

With the continued existence of every business hinging on the development of new leaders to carry on, one would expect that American business generally would have a well-organized and well-planned attack on the job of providing executive leaders. Unfortunately, even a systematic search does not disclose many companies with an effective program for developing their own future executives and leaders. Of course, a few score of companies have well-organized executive development programs; for the most part, these are the larger and more successful concerns. But to date, most American companies have left the development of their future executives on an unplanned basis.

Of course, that does not mean that a substantial amount of executive development is not going on all the time in American business concerns. Businessmen recognize generally that the production of profits depends largely on the ability of the personnel of the enterprise and especially of its executive personnel. For that reason, most companies do some informal executive development. Most executives will admit that developing understudies is an important part of every executive's job, and most of them do something about it.

In the conduct of several million enterprises, naturally executives also have a great opportunity to develop into leaders through experience. There is much on-the-job learning and some on-the-job coaching of subordinates by superiors.

Much executive development also originates with the individual. In view of the great opportunity for advancement in American business, a man with ambition and initiative will learn how to be an executive and then a leader — even though his company has no organized program for training him to be either. Every man who enters business knows that if his company follows the policies that produce the greatest profits, he has an opportunity some day to head the business.

Outstanding business leaders — recognizing the major executive development job to be done — are not satisfied to leave the job to these natural forces. They know that American business can do any job better with good organization and effective planning. These leaders are putting the development of executive leadership on an organized basis in their own companies and are using their influence to encourage other companies to employ the same attack.

### THE BUSINESS LEADER'S "OUTSIDE" RESPONSIBILITIES

An increasing number of progressive business leaders realize that today their responsibilities extend beyond the office or plant door. They are trying to educate their employees to see the close identity between their individual interests and the interests of the enterprise which employs them. They know that the well-informed employee will not cast a vote that creates an unfavorable atmosphere for business; for if he is well informed, he recognizes that, in an industrialized economy such as ours, what is good for business is good for the greatest number of citizens generally.

Far-sighted business leaders are also aware of their responsibility to assist employees in broadening their understanding of economics and in gaining an understanding of how the vitality of our economy depends on risk-taking and on preserving public attitudes that encourage opportunity rather than a retreat to security.

These factors were given official recognition in the recent statement (August 8, 1949) prepared by Thomas B. McCabe, Chairman of the Federal Reserve Board, at the request of a Senate Banking and Currency subcommittee. In his statement Mr. McCabe said, "Security rather than opportunity has become more and more a part of our national philosophy." Deploring the growth of this viewpoint, Mr. McCabe also stressed that "risk-taking had long been an American tradition. It resulted in the rapid development of our resources, expanding production, and a steadily rising standard of living."

Far-sighted business leaders recognize their responsibility — in the interests of business and the nation as a whole — to bring home to their employees the importance of public attitudes that result in risk-taking and the preservation of opportunity for the individual.

Business leaders who have thought deeply about the problem of public economic education have concluded that they have responsibilities which extend beyond the education of their own employees. They realize that employee economic education can be diluted and even nullified by influences in the community. Consequently, these leaders are participating in activities outside their companies. These activities look toward a broader understanding of the needs of business if it is to continue to give our country a constantly rising standard of living, which is by all odds the highest the world has ever known.

### SOURCE AND MAKE-UP OF THE BOOK

It was against this background of the problems of business leadership that the Alumni Conference Committee of the Harvard Business School Association planned the annual conference devoted to major business topics of current significance. The various sections of this book are based on speeches the authors made at the Nineteenth Annual Conference of the Harvard Business School Association held June 11, 1949 at Harvard Graduate School of Business Administration, Soldiers Field, Boston. The introduction by Dean David is based on a speech to the Economic Club of Detroit, published as a supplement to the *Harvard Business Review,* May 1949.

This volume is a companion to the report of the Eighteenth Annual Conference of the Association, held in 1948. The Proceedings of the Eighteenth Conference were published by the Harvard University Press under the title *The Responsibilities of Business Leadership.* The present volume describes how business can develop leaders who are equipped to discharge the responsibilities dealt with in the 1948 Conference.

Each of the authors selected by our Committee is a demonstrated leader in his own field. Each has thought deeply about his particular phase of the subject. Several have had an opportunity, in the companies which they head, to practice the principles they discuss.

The material divides itself logically into two parts. Part I — "The Kind of Business Leaders We Need" — treats the problems business leaders face and must be prepared to deal with. Included are discussions of economic and social trends affecting the business leader's activities; the job he has to do internally; and his tasks as a citizen and member of his community.

Part II — "Steps in Developing the Kind of Business

Leaders We Need"—presents concrete material by the heads of three corporations on the steps they are taking to develop executives in their companies. This part concludes with specific suggestions on how the individual can get ahead in business.

I have prepared a brief introductory note to each section which includes biographical information about the author.

I believe that this book will be of interest and of concrete value to business leaders, to those who aspire to business leadership, and to the young man eager to get ahead in business. The authors define precisely the opportunities that business leaders have for increasing the effectiveness of their own concerns and improving the general climate for business. They also give specific, step-by-step suggestions that any business leader can follow in his own business, his own community, and in the development of his own career.

MARVIN BOWER

*New York City*
*August 15, 1949*

## CONTENTS

# INTRODUCTION

DONALD KIRK DAVID

The world we live in is a battleground upon which the adversaries are democracy and totalitarianism. The conflict is one of social systems — of methods through which society makes its decisions in social, political, and economic affairs. The weapons which are in use are military, political, economic, intellectual, and even religious. The test of these systems will lie in their effectiveness in attaining the satisfactions — material, human, and spiritual — which are the goals of any society. This war of methods and ideas gives rise to new problems, and it underscores older ones with which we are already familiar; it is the source of the greatest uncertainties of our world.

## ROLE OF THE BUSINESS LEADER

In this struggle I am deeply convinced that the democratic side is right, and I am confident that it will prevail. It will not be an easy struggle. Victory will be obtained neither cheaply nor quickly. Yet I am sure that we shall tread the path successfully, that we shall meet the challenges of the present and those of the future. And in the achievement of this victory I know that responsible business leadership has a role of major proportions as we make our way through the uncertainties that surround us.

The effective businessman has, it seems to me, two special abilities. He is skilled in the art and science of the purposeful organization of men and things. He is also trained in the taking of risks and the facing of uncertainties. He makes his decisions and carries out his actions after a considered appraisal of the risks involved. These twin capacities — purposeful organization and the exercise of judgment leading to action — are needed today as never before. These abilities which have been developed to a high degree within individual business units are the basis of the contribution which responsible business leadership can and must make to our society in its attempt to work its way through the troubled present and the uncertain future.

In such a world, it seems to me, these special attributes of the businessman are required not less but more. That this is true of the art of administration hardly needs emphasis, since in an increasingly complex and specialized world the effective organization of men and things in large units is an obvious essential. But it is the second special capacity of the businessman — his unique training in facing uncertainty, evaluating risks, and exercising judgment leading to action — that seems to me particularly relevant.

### THE BUSINESS LEADER'S FIRST TASK

I feel strongly that operating a successful business is the first responsibility of a business leader. The simple fact is that in our society the businessman is primarily responsible for organizing the production and distribution of the nation's goods and services. He can meet that responsibility only through the competent management of business enterprise and through the creation and development of healthy business concerns. To me it is unrealistic to presume that the business leader can discharge any other responsibility if he fails in this, his foremost job. And in this area the most important asset of the business leader is his training and experience in the taking of calculated risks.

GETTING PEOPLE TO WORK TOGETHER

Part of the businessman's competence lies in his ability to get people to work together for a common goal. It is here, as I see it, that the second responsibility of business leadership arises — the responsibility for making his organization a "good society." Businessmen have known for a long time — almost instinctively — that the people under them had to "work together." Many, however, knew little and cared less how those people felt so long as the business "got results," that is, produced economic satisfactions.

We know very little of human motivations, and we need to know more because here, I am convinced, is one key to the problems which confront us. We do know, however, that the area is tricky and one can easily get snarled up in words. For instance, one hears much these days about giving employees "a sense of participation." In our observation this is not enough. The participation must be real. Or at least the opportunity to participate must be real. It must come from a genuine recognition by the leader that each member of his organization has something to contribute to it and needs to be given the opportunity to do so. The business leader, then, must believe in the dignity of the individual and in the value of each man's participation.

### A BUSINESS AS A SOCIAL UNIT

At this point I want to make clear that I am not speaking of just the top men in industry, of just the top operating executives, but of almost every member of a business organization. The responsibility for competence and the responsibility for creation of a good society fall — in varying degree, of course — upon every person who has a directive part, no matter how small, in the activities of the people that make up the organization. A business is more than an economic unit; it is a social unit as well — or, rather, a group of interrelated social units of varying sizes. Thus each business executive — each foreman and supervisor — is within certain limits guiding a small society.

At the same time the leader of one of these units is a participant in a larger organization. His performance in that larger group depends substantially upon the degree of participation he has been able to encourage from those who make up the social unit of which he is the head. Thus, it is through the exercise of his skills — his administrative talent and his competence in judging risks and taking wise actions — within the framework of the social unit with which he is directly concerned that the business executive is enabled to make a contribution to the larger unit of which he is a part.

### PARTICIPATION IN PUBLIC AFFAIRS

Now I have emphasized this concept because I think it is useful when we come to examine a third quality which I believe necessary to a business leader, namely, his constructive participation in the broader affairs of his community and nation.

There is a parallelism, it seems to me, between the problems of a business organization trying to survive and to provide satisfactions for its members in the face of changing uncertainties and the problems of our society faced as it is with the larger uncertainties of the totalitarian challenge and the possibility of atomic warfare. And I believe I see important similarities between the way in which a business executive makes his contribution to his company and the way in which responsible business leadership may make a contribution to our society.

If I am right in viewing the problems which face our society as requiring the calculation of the risks involved, the formulation of a program to be carried out, and the effective administration of that program, then I cannot see why the business leader should feel himself upon unfamiliar ground when he participates in the affairs of his community and nation. We have already seen that the special talents of the businessman are developed in the handling of problems with just these elements, albeit on a smaller scale. And now that our civilization stands in need of talents such as I have described, I am more convinced than ever that responsible business leadership has a great contribution to make in the years that lie ahead.

This conviction that our society demands ever more effective participation from business leaders is shared, I know, by businessmen throughout the country. At the same time it is recognized by leaders in many other fields — education, the church, the legal profession — yes, even by leaders in government and the labor movement. The great problem, however, lies in finding ways to carry out this conviction in our daily activities. In this area there are no easy answers or ready solutions but I am greatly impressed with the ever-growing interest of businessmen in learning methods and exchanging ideas as to how they can provide greater opportunities for men and women to draw satisfaction from their daily work.

Even more encouraging is the growing concern of businessmen with the problem of making effective contributions to the management of public affairs. In my opinion the way in which the businessman approaches this problem is of extreme importance. We all know that our sprawling and dynamic society is no simple matter. It is made up of the utmost diversity of human beings and social groupings subject to strains, tensions, and frustrations in their mutual relations. We know so little about human motives and the forces which govern human relationships. In recent years these problems have become increasingly the subject of organized research, research which promises growing understanding. But only a beginning has been made. Psychology, sociology, social anthropology — all show promise of contributing substantial help.

Those of us concerned with business should remember that business is only one among many of the loosely organized sectors in the society; it plays its part alongside others such as agriculture, labor, government, and the various professions. The problems to be solved are formidable, and no one can rightly claim to know all the answers. The methods to be used are often beyond the businessman's experience within his own operating unit. But, however novel the problems or the ways of dealing with them, the truly effective businessman retains his capacity to learn and his ability to provide leadership. He shows a readiness to recognize and benefit from diversity of opinion. Surely he is entitled to take a legitimate pride in the special capacities which stem from his business training and experience, but he knows that business has no monopoly of brains or skills or even courage to face up to uncertainties, and that effective solutions can be achieved only with the full expression and resolution of diverse opinions.

### "TOUGH-MINDED HUMILITY"

In my observation, those businessmen who have been most effective in public affairs — those who, in a word, have been true business leaders in this complex world — all share certain attitudes and characteristics in addition to competence. First and foremost, these men exhibit what I like to call "tough-minded humility." The tough-mindedness is essential to competent handling of these complex problems and flows from that training and experience in calculated risk-taking and decisive judgment which I have stressed. But the humility is of equal importance. It flows from a recognition of the complexities of the problems and the fact that many diverse backgrounds and talents must be brought to bear upon their solution. I am convinced that the public over a period of time does not respond to intolerant, dogmatic, or imperious leadership in politics, in labor, or in business.

EXECUTIVE DEVELOPMENT

Obviously much more is involved in the development of executive leadership than just this matter of attitude and approach. The thoughtful reader of this book will find, I am sure, many suggestions and ideas of practical and positive worth as he goes about his daily task of building an organization and exercising judgment in the direction of its activities. At the same time I hope he will find inspiration and encouragement to face the larger problem of participation in public affairs as well as ideas that will broaden and stimulate his thinking and activity in these matters. I am convinced that the executive leadership we need to develop for the future must be based on an approach that is neither biased nor oversimplified, and must be built around an attitude that is both vigorous and adaptable.

Development of executive leadership of this sort is in my opinion the greatest opportunity facing American businessmen. Like all opportunities it is also a challenge, for it is clear to me that failure to develop greater and more effective participation of business leadership in the management of public affairs will greatly diminish the ability of democracy to succeed in the conflict with totalitarianism.

# PART I

# The Kind of Business Leaders We Need

# THE PROBLEMS OF BUSINESS LEADERSHIP IN A LABORISTIC ECONOMY

BY

*Sumner H. Slichter*

LAMONT UNIVERSITY PROFESSOR

HARVARD UNIVERSITY

CAMBRIDGE, MASSACHUSETTS

The leader has ability to detect and understand external conditions affecting the welfare of the group he is leading and the foresight to adapt the activities of the group to changed conditions. Under today's unsettled and complex economic and social conditions, the leader of any business group is taxed severely in the exercise of these aspects of leadership.

Any executive today who aspires to attain or hold business leadership must give penetrating and thoughtful consideration to external conditions affecting the internal operations of the business. And clearly, this phase of the exercise of leadership is a more demanding one in any period of war, social unrest, and basically changing economic conditions. The executive who can understand these external changes and interpret them to his enterprise and assist it in adapting its activities to external factors is certainly entitled to leadership consideration.

The writings of Dr. Sumner Slichter, one of the nation's leading economists, have been aiding business leaders in these respects for many years. He combines a penetrating insight of economic forces with the ability to interpret them lucidly to the layman. In addition, he has long been a student of the labor movement and of social forces affecting business operations.

This unusual combination of abilities qualifies Dr. Slichter exceptionally well to assist business leaders and executives in identifying and understanding the external forces affecting their enterprises and their individual responsibilities. In this first section of the book, Dr. Slichter gives a clear and thorough analysis of these external forces and takes a long look ahead in a way that should be particularly useful to business leaders. His analysis will aid them in their efforts to adapt their enterprises to changing conditions and will also aid them in understanding and discharging their personal responsibilities and opportunities as business leaders during the next decade.

In addition to his teaching at Harvard University and the Harvard Graduate School of Business Administration, Dr. Slichter finds time to speak to important business groups and to contribute frequently to the *New York Times Magazine*. His most recent books are *The American Economy; Challenge of Industrial Relations: Trade Unions, Management and the Public Interest;* and *Trade Unions in a Free Society*. In June 1949 Harvard University and his alma mater, the University of Wisconsin, gave him honorary degrees in recognition of his work in his field.

## THE PROBLEMS OF BUSINESS LEADERSHIP IN A LABORISTIC ECONOMY

Few periods in the world's history have seen so many important changes as has the last century. Especially during the last fifty years have occurred three changes of great importance to management. One is the transformation of the economy from one of free private enterprise to one of government-guided enterprise. A second is the rise of the welfare state. A third is the shift of power from business to employees.

These three changes, and especially the shift in power from business to employees, require that business managers consider what is happening to their position in the community. Should business managers seek to resist the basic trends which have developed in the last fifty years? Should they oppose these trends? Should they seek to guide or modify them? Should they pursue one policy toward some trends and other policies toward others? In a laboristic community such as has developed, can business managers hope to have much influence upon policies? What interest does the community have in the policies adopted by business managers toward basic economic and political trends? These are the questions to which I wish to address myself.

## DEVELOPMENT OF BASIC CHANGES IN THE ECONOMY

Let me begin by discussing briefly the three basic changes that have occurred.

1. *The transformation of the economy from one of free enterprise to government-guided enterprise.* Back in the nineteenth century most people believed that the economy could be trusted to run itself, because, if capital and labor were free to move from one industry to another, the economy would produce what people desired it to make and competition would keep prices down and quality up. This belief had much validity. Nevertheless, the community has been more and more refusing to accept the results of free markets. I shall not go into the reasons behind the revolt against the free market. The principal reason, I think, has been that under a democracy various groups are bound to use their political power to gain economic advantage. Another reason has been that under free markets the economy tended to grow too fast with the result that the foundation was laid for a subsequent contraction.

At any rate, first here and then there the community has sought to substitute public policies for the uncontrolled results of markets. Fifty years of revolt against the results produced by free markets has gradually transformed the economy from one of free enterprise into one of government-guided enterprise. Today the community expects the government to put a floor under some prices, a ceiling over others; to subsidize this industry, to put special taxes on that one; to regulate the terms on which money is lent and to some extent the purposes for which it is lent; to lend money itself; and to modify drastically the distribution of income by a combination of steeply progressive income taxes and large transfer payments. These changes have come so gradually that many people have failed to notice the fundamental transformation that has been taking place.

There is still much room, of course, for individual decisions to determine what shall be purchased, what shall be made, and what methods of production shall be used. These decisions are made, however, within the framework of an increasingly elaborate set of government rules. Let there be no mistake, therefore, that a revolution has occurred in the economy of the United States, and that it is still going on.

The present economy is quite different from free private enterprise and is based on a different principle. Free private enterprise operated on the principle that ability and willingness to buy determined what was produced and who got it. The new economy operates on the principle that fundamental decisions on who has what incomes, what is produced, and at what prices it is sold are determined by public policies. Ten years from now the framework of government rules and public policies will be more elaborate than it is today and will limit the discretion of management at many more points.

2. *The development of the welfare state, or possibly the handout state.* The essential principle of the welfare state is that incomes should not be tied too closely to contributions to production. There are many millions of people in the community who have great needs but who are not able to work. There are others who are not able to hold

full-time jobs unless they give up important activities, such as getting an education.

During the last 15 or 20 years the attitude of the community toward needs has greatly changed. Today the community is prepared to go much farther than ever before in disbursing income on the basis of need. Within the last 15 years the United States has instituted a system of old age pensions which covers about three out of five jobs and a system of unemployment compensation which covers about seven out of ten employees. It has also increased greatly the opportunities for free public education. In 1929 payments based on need were about $1.2 billion and represented about 1.2 per cent of all personal incomes; in 1948, such payments were over $11.1 billion and represented about 5.2 per cent of all personal incomes. In 1948, payments based on need were 40 per cent greater than the dividend disbursements of all American corporations.

Payments based on need, however, are still small in relation to need. For example, the average pension under old age and survivors' insurance is about $26 a month in the case of persons without dependents and $39 a month in the case of persons with dependents. Disability payments are meager. Within a decade, payments based on need will be far larger than now — in fact, they will probably be running close to $20 billion a year.

It remains to be seen whether the community will develop a welfare state in which legitimate needs will be met through social insurance and through relief administered free from political influence or whether the policy of relieving the needy will become an instrument of politics so that the community develops a handout state rather than a welfare state. The danger that the community may develop a handout state is indicated by experience with old age relief. In the state of Louisiana approximately eight out of ten persons 65 years of age or over are receiving old age assistance; in two other states the proportion is more than five out of ten; and in five other states, more than four out of ten. In states such as New Jersey or New York, where administration is stricter, the proportion is less than one out of ten.

3. *The shift in power from business to employees.* During the nineteenth century the most influential single group in the community was undoubtedly the businessmen. During the last fifty years the influence of businessmen in the community has been slowly declining. Evidence of this shift is found in the history of legislation. Most major pieces of legislation, such as the Federal Reserve Act, the Income Tax, the Clayton Act, the Norris-La Guardia Act, the Securities and Exchange Act, the Wagner Act, and the Social Security Act, were adopted either in the face of opposition from the predominant part of the business community or without much participation by businessmen in the formulation of the legislation. Some important laws, it is true, were drafted with participation by business groups or passed with support of a large part of the business community. Examples are some workmen's compensation laws, the Railway Labor Act of 1926, the Fair Labor Standards Act, and the Taft-Hartley Act. Nevertheless, it is plain, I think, that the influence of businessmen in the community has been diminishing.

The basic reason for the shift in power from businessmen to employees is the increase in the relative number of employees. In the early part of the nineteenth century the community was made up predominantly of self-employed persons. Today, however, over three out of four persons who work for a living in the United States are on someone else's payroll.

The shift of power to employees has been aided by two conditions — by the rapid organization of employees and by the unwillingness of businessmen to go very far in offering constructive proposals for dealing with the problems which have emerged. In the United States today, about 15 million employees are organized into trade unions through which the ideas of employees on public and business policies receive expression. The unwillingness of businessmen to offer constructive solutions to problems is well illustrated by the development of policies for compensating the unemployed. Some way of giving relief to the unemployed is obviously necessary. Businessmen were scornful of schemes for unemployment insurance, which were labeled "the dole" and were reputed to undermine the will to work. Businessmen for the most part held that the responsibility for relief should be assumed by each separate community — despite the fact that localities having in the main capital goods industries could not assume the heavy cost of relief for many months. When the great depression of the thirties developed, businessmen attempted to relieve unemployment by putting on a "spread-the-work" movement — useful as far as it went but far from adequate. The failure of businessmen to take the lead in providing the country with satisfactory arrangements for compensating unemployment caused policies in this field to be made by non-business groups.

Essentially the same thing happened in other fields. Had business leaders been willing to demand legislation against the abuses which eventually led to the passage of the Securities and Exchange Act, the law would have been written five or ten years earlier with the help of businessmen and the country would have obtained better balanced and more practical legislation.

The weak position of business in policy-making is best indicated by an examination of the outlook for new laws and policies. The critics of the economy have a large inventory of unexecuted proposals. No comparable inventory of projects is sponsored by the business community. This means that the intellectual initiative in the community has largely passed from businessmen to others. Business has enough influence to defeat in any year most of the new proposals. Hence business *seems* to be very influential—it wins a large part of the battles over policy, perhaps most of them. Each year, however, there are adopted a few policies and laws which businessmen do not like. In the course of ten years the economy is substantially changed in ways that business has opposed. Hence, although business is winning a large part of the battles, it is losing the campaign.

## NEEDED INFLUENCES OF BUSINESS MANAGERS

The shift in power from business to labor has, on the whole, been good for the community. It has made policy-makers better informed and caused them to become concerned with a broader range of problems, including some problems which received little attention when business interests were dominant. The shift in power is also causing many accepted practices, policies, and institutions to be challenged and reconsidered. It is always a good thing for the community to take a fresh look at long-established practices and institutions.

Although the shift of power has done much good, I believe that it has gone too far and that the community would be better off if business managers recovered some of their lost influence. Business managers as a general rule are interested in different things from employees, and see problems that employees overlook. Hence businessmen have important contributions to make to public policies. Let me give a few specific illustrations of fields in which business might make important and distinctive contributions to thinking about policies.

1. *The need of the community for more production.* The outlook for production is bright. If output per manhour increases at 2 per cent a year (slightly more than the average rate in the past) and the length of the workweek drops by one-fourth, and the proportion of the population in the labor force remains unchanged, production per capita per year will reach $2377 (in terms of 1948 dollars) by 1980, or $8500 per family. With a population of about 175 million, the national income will be about $416 billion. Industrial research is growing by leaps and bounds. And the tremendous research program of the government will yield important help to industry. Consequently output may increase by as much as 3 per cent per manhour per year. If that happens and if the workweek drops by one-fourth, per capita annual income will be $3252 by 1980 and the national income $569 billion.

Even a rise in output of 3 per cent per manhour per

year is none too favorable for a community which has assumed the major responsibility for keeping the world at peace, halting the spread of communism, building up backward areas, and at the same time operating a welfare state which distributes billions of dollars on the basis of need and which has by far the most powerful labor movement which the world has ever seen. Unions are not likely to be content with raising wages no more than 2 per cent or 3 per cent a year. Consequently, unless there is an offsetting rise in prices, the wage demands of unions alone would absorb the entire increase in the national product during the next thirty years, and leave none for these other needs.

It is plain that production needs to be encouraged. Most groups in the community are not much interested in production. Their concern is with the distribution of income. Their proposals usually relate to ways of changing distribution. Business groups cannot always be depended upon to support proposals for increasing the productive capacity of the community. Influential business groups have opposed bringing Texas gas to the East or opening up the St. Lawrence waterway or establishing a Columbia River authority. By and large, however, business managers are the most reliable and most consistent friends of more production in the community. Hence an increase in the influence of businessmen upon policy would help the community meet the need for an enormous increase in output.

2. *The interest of the community in accumulating capital.* The rate of saving in the future is likely to be sufficient to supply the community with ample capital provided conditions of investment are reasonably favorable. In the

past, more than half of the savings of the community have been needed to provide housing, plant, and equipment for the rapidly growing population. The prospect that population will increase less than 25 per cent in the next 30 years indicates that a much lower rate of saving will make possible a given rise in capital per worker.

The population of the country, it is true, may increase faster than the experts predict — at any rate the growth of population has recently been outrunning the forecasts. Furthermore, even if the volume of savings is ample, conditions may not be favorable for getting equity capital directly from individual investors.

One might expect that a progressive and dynamic community, such as the United States with its strong pioneering traditions, would show special favor to equity capital — the most productive type of capital. The opposite, however, is true. The community imposes on income from equity corporate capital an extra 38 per cent tax which no other kind of income, whether from property or services, has to pay. Consequently it is plain that equity capital needs friends. No one has better reason to champion the cause of equity capital than the trade unions, but the interest of unions in the increase in equity capital is a long-run interest. Thus far unions have not shown much capacity to give attention to long-run matters. The business managers seem to be one group in the community which can be best depended upon to champion the cause of equity capital. This is another reason why an increase in their influence would be helpful to the community.

3. *The interest of the community in price movements as regulators of economic activity.* I have indicated that in

the last two generations the community has gone quite far in rejecting the results of markets, and in limiting the extent to which price movements determine what is produced and in what quantities. There is danger that the community will go too far in regulating prices, that it will respond too easily to the pressure of special groups, and will fail to let general considerations of public policy have much to do with decisions about particular markets.

Prices are by no means a perfect regulator of economic activities, but they do possess important merits. When they are not permitted to determine the allocation of resources and the rate of production, an elaborate set of controls is necessary. There is also danger that price controls will produce many unintended effects. For example, some of the proposals to regulate farm prices would actually unstabilize farm incomes.

Certainly the country needs persons who understand the merits of price movements as organizers of production and who are able to champion in an intelligent way the interests of the community in free prices. Business managers cannot be depended upon *always* to provide intelligent and understanding championship of prices as regulators of economic activity. Nevertheless, business managers are the group in the community from which such championship is most likely to come. Consequently, an increase in the influence of businessmen on policy will help the community to develop good arrangements for getting resources allocated among different industries and regions and for providing effective incentives for capacity to be expanded where there is demand for it.

4. *The interest of the community in the economic conse-*

*quences of collective bargaining.* With collective bargaining as pervasive as it is, its consequences are bound to affect profoundly the operation of the economy. Hence it is important that the community develop wise criteria to guide the process of wage setting under collective bargaining. This means the creation of a new body of thought — a body of thought so well worked out that it commands rather general acceptance.

Thus far union representatives have maintained that virtually every kind of situation calls for a wage increase — although there are some exceptions to this observation. For example, unions pretty generally have argued that both inflation and deflation call for wage increases. The stand of employers has been pretty consistently against wage increases regardless of conditions.

Perhaps the only way in which the community can develop a body of thought about wages is through this clash of opinion between unions and employers — unions always insisting that a wage increase is needed and employers always insisting that it is not called for. This process, however, does not impress me as well adapted for producing a good quality of thinking about wages. There is need for more discriminating and more judicial thinking. Can business managers begin to supply it? I am not sure. It is not an easy kind of thinking to do. Furthermore, it seems to require a certain amount of detachment. Nevertheless, here is an opportunity for business managers and trade union leaders as well to make important contributions to the community's ideas about wages.

5. *The development of a set of mores to guide behavior in the field of industrial relations.* The rapid rise of unions

in the last 15 years confronts the community overnight with many new problems of social control. So long as unions were small and weak, they could be treated in the main as private clubs. Furthermore, the failure of unions to reach agreements with employers did not as a rule result in serious injury to the community, and the terms of agreement between unions and employers did not much matter.

I shall not attempt to enumerate the many problems which have been created by the rise of unions. Some of them relate to the internal affairs of unions. Others relate to limiting the area of industrial disputes and protecting neutrals from being forced by one party or the other to become participants in an industrial dispute. Still others relate to the problem of protecting the community against the interruption of vital services. It is clear that the field of industrial relations cannot be left to laissez faire. Conduct in this area must be guided either by ethical codes or by laws — probably by a mixture of the two. The idea of restraint upon union activities is extremely obnoxious to some union leaders. This should not be surprising — businessmen felt the same way toward proposals to impose new obligations on railroads, banks, municipal utilities, and the securities business.

Here is another area where the development of wise policies requires penetrating and discriminating thinking — thinking guided by concern for the interests of the community and the desire to make collective bargaining operate satisfactorily. Perhaps neither businessmen nor trade union leaders are capable of rising above narrow partisanship in their thinking about problems of labor relations. I think, however, that they can do much better than they have thus far done in the discussions of the issues raised by the Taft-Hartley Act. Those who are able and willing to do first-class thinking will have much influence on the kind of ethical code and system of jurisprudence which the community develops to make the conduct of industrial relations correspond to the public interest.

### HOW BUSINESS MANAGERS CAN INCREASE THEIR INFLUENCE

There are three principal ways in which business managers can increase their influence in a laboristic community. The first is by making business a more integral part of the community. The second is by doing first-rate thinking. The third is by taking a greater and broader interest in the problems of the community.

When I suggest that business needs to become a more integral part of the community, I am referring to the corporate part of industry. The 6 million enterprises in agriculture and the 3.5 million unincorporated concerns outside of agriculture are pretty much a part of the community. This is not true, however, of American corporate industry as a whole. And yet corporations produce roughly half of the national income and about 57 per cent of that part of national income produced by all private enterprise.* They pay about 64 per cent of all wages and salaries in the United States and 75 per cent of all wages and salaries paid by private industry. Corporations employ about two-thirds of all of the employees engaged in private industry, about 55 per cent of all employees, public

* In computing this percentage, I have eliminated corporate income tax liability from the total national income.

and private, and around 45 per cent of all gainfully employed persons, including the self-employed.

Corporations, however, are owned by a fairly small part of the population — apparently by about six or seven million shareholders. The net investment of individuals in corporations has increased very little during the last fifteen years. Only a small part of individual savings goes into corporate securities. During the years 1933 to 1941, when personal savings were $24.9 billion, individuals *reduced* their investment in corporate stocks and bonds by $2.38 billion. During the years 1946 to 1948, inclusive, when personal savings were $27.4 billion, individuals increased their investments in corporate stocks and bonds by only $3.5 billion, or less than one-seventh of their savings.*

Back in 1933 there were over two stockholders in American corporations for every member of a trade union. Union membership has increased five times while the number of stockholders has changed little. Today there are over two union members for every stockholder. Obviously, corporations are in a precarious position in a laboristic community when their stockholders constitute only a small fraction of the adult population. Even more disturbing than this is the fact that the number of stockholders shows little tendency to increase.

I do not propose to discuss the complicated problem of how corporations may take root in the community and become a part of it. Part of the solution of the problem, I believe, must be achieved through a great increase in the

* *Survey of Current Business*, Special Supplement, July 1947, p. 20; July, 1949, pp. 10, 11.

number of stockholders. This means that millions of persons with small incomes must be persuaded to become shareholders in American corporations. This in turn means that corporations must offer a type of security which may be appropriately owned by persons with small incomes to whom security of principal is very important.

Part of the solution of the problem must be worked out also in other ways. It is important, I believe, that the boards of directors become more representative of a cross section of the community and include more leaders of opinion and persons who have first-hand information about problems of the community — editors, farmers, professional men, small businessmen, and even preachers. At present the directorates of most corporations consist almost entirely of officials of other corporations, plus a few so-called "capitalists" — that is, men who own large investments but who do not directly administer enterprises. The directorates do not as a rule include many leaders of the community from outside the business world and even from the agricultural or small-business segments of business.

The assumption has apparently been that only corporate officials, bankers, or large investors are competent to make the kind of decisions which directors have to make. For most questions which come before boards this assumption is probably correct, and I do not believe that non-businessmen should be a majority on any board of directors. I would not care to own stock in a company which was being run by amateurs. Nevertheless, in a laboristic society the boards of directors of corporations need to be more representative of the community than the present boards, partly in order to help the managements of corporations understand the viewpoints of the community and partly in order to give community leaders an insight into the way corporations are run and the problems which they encounter. Although I would not care to own stock in a company dominated by non-businessmen, my interests as a stockholder would be better served in the long run if boards of directors were more representative. This is simply a somewhat personal way of asserting that in a community where corporations produce half of the goods and where the philosophy of the people is democratic it is not desirable that the directors of corporations consist almost exclusively of officers of other corporations.

The second way in which business leaders may affect the course of events is by their influence upon ideas. Ideas have always been important in the course of history — as witness the effect of the idea of the infinite worth of the individual upon the development of civilization in Western Europe. Of consequence in more recent years is the Marxian idea that the essential relationship between men is one of conflict and that history consists of a struggle between economic classes.

Competition between ideas is stiff and will probably get stiffer, as conditions of communication improve. This is a wholesome state of affairs. I shall not undertake a rounded discussion of what determines whether or not an idea has much influence. Ideas may receive wide acceptance in some fields without having the support of evidence. This is particularly true in those fields where evidence is unobtainable or where men tend to do wishful thinking. Ideas about the hereafter are an example.

Many ideas gain influence, however, because they *are*

supported by evidence or because they seem to promise solution to important and baffling problems. Ideas appear to be particularly influential if they relate to problems which concern a large part of the community. Furthermore, ideas gain influence when they are positive rather than negative. If the community has a difficult and persistent problem and wishes to do something about it, the people who do not go beyond indicating objections to each and every proposal will probably have only limited influence. The community will insist on doing something. The people who have most influence upon events are those who are willing to propose solutions to problems.

Can business develop men who are able to make important contributions to thinking? Is it not asking the impossible to expect men to be both able administrators and important thinkers in the field of public policy? How can men find time both to manage an enterprise in a highly competitive and rapidly changing economy and to become sufficiently well informed in the fields of economics, political science, sociology, and other disciplines to do first-class thinking in the field of public policy?

I realize that I am proposing a stiff task. Bear in mind that I do not assert that *every* administrator must be an important thinker in the field of public policy. I simply assert that business needs to contribute its fair share of the important thinkers of the age. Business has the choice of letting public policy be made pretty exclusively by critics of the economy or of developing some executives who are capable of competing successfully with other thinkers and winning acceptance for a fair share of their ideas.

That business *can* develop important and influential

thinkers is indicated by the fact that it has already done so. I could mention names if I had to. The development of executives who are interested and well informed about problems of public policy will be assisted if business organizations appreciate the worth of such men and encourage their development. Not every man who is an able executive is well qualified by temperament, interest, or ability to make important contributions to thought. When an enterprise discovers that it has an executive who is able to do first-class thinking in the field of public policy, it should encourage him to do this regardless of whether or not his ideas happen to conform with the ideas of the board of directors or his superiors. Important thinking is likely to have important elements of nonconformity.

Arrangements can be worked out which help businessmen to become well informed and which help them to develop ideas. The methods of the Committee for Economic Development are an example. These methods include a general research committee which is a deliberative and arguing body and subcommittees which are also deliberative and arguing but which work on specific problems. The methods also include special research studies which are made available to the subcommittees and the general research committee as the basis for policy statements. The methods of the C.E.D. also include attaching special technicians to the subcommittees both as participants in the discussion and as drafters of policy statements. I do not suggest that policy statements issued by committees represent the best quality of thought that businessmen might do on public issues. These statements sometimes suffer from compromises. Nevertheless, the process of working out these policy statements develops the ideas of the makers of the policy statement and helps each one of them do well-informed, individual, and forthright thinking.

The third way in which business leaders may increase their influence upon policy is by taking a greater and broader interest in the problems of the community. The success of business in producing important thinkers will do little good unless business enjoys the confidence and the good will of the community. Otherwise its spokesmen cannot get much of a hearing.

Recently businessmen have had reason to complain of the hostile environment in which they do business. A typical statement is one by Mr. G. W. Price, President of the Westinghouse Electric Company. He describes as "the most alarming symptom and the most dangerous condition the fact that American business is now operating in a climate so hostile to enterprise that it is unable to obtain its capital requirements from the investing public." *

This statement raises very basic questions for business. Apparently the author does not regard business as having much reponsibility for its environment. *But why did the climate become hostile to enterprise?* What did business do or fail to do that permitted the environment to become hostile?

Part of the explanation undoubtedly is the great depression of the thirties. Part of it, however, has been the failure of businessmen to take much interest in the problems of the community, and their tendency to oppose proposals for dealing with these problems without offering alternative

* *Wall Street Journal*, April 15, 1949, p. 3.

constructive suggestions. Much of the opposition of business to the attempts of the community to solve its problems was quite unnecessary. Even from the standpoint of its own narrow special interests business would have been wise to demand proper factory legislation instead of opposing it. It might well have insisted upon adequate arrangements for unemployment compensation or demanded adequate old age pensions. But surely in a community composed mainly of employees it was a blunder for business to fight a bitter war against unions regardless of whether or not employees wished to have unions.

I am not sure that even today business leaders realize the importance of showing a broad concern for the problems of the community. Recently I was amazed to read the testimony of a representative of the American Bankers' Association before a committee of Congress, opposing the renewal of the present authority of the Federal Reserve Board over consumer credit. Nothing undermines the position of business in a community more than does a depression. Hence all branches of business have a vital interest in keeping business stable. Limiting the growth of consumer credit during periods of expansion must be part of a general program for stabilizing business. Perhaps there is a better way of controlling consumer credit than through the Federal Reserve System — though I do not know of one. The essential point is that business cannot afford to adopt a merely negative position toward the control of consumer credit.

I was also astonished recently to read a talk by the president of a large corporation against making the Federal Social Security system more adequate. The system is pathetically inadequate at the present time. If there is anything which a vigorous and dynamic society needs it is an adequate and comprehensive arrangement for compensation of persons who have retired or who are unemployed. Business can gain the confidence and the good will of the community by showing an understanding of its problems and by helping to find solutions. If its leaders are uninformed about these problems, if they are not interested in them, and if they discuss them only for the purpose of opposing this or that proposed "solution," the influence of business in the community will be small.

## PROSPECTS THAT BUSINESS WILL REGAIN SOME OF ITS LOST INFLUENCE

Is there really much chance for business leaders to exert substantial influence in a laboristic community? Is it not preposterous to expect them to do this? Are not business managers so hopelessly outnumbered that their chances for exerting substantial influence are virtually nil?

It is my judgment that the chances that business will succeed in winning back a substantial part of its lost influence are fairly good, but not bright. I believe that corporations will gradually succeed in taking root in the community and becoming a part of it. That will not be easily accomplished, and many businessmen are not yet ready to concede the importance of attempting to do it. Nevertheless, I think that the need for much broader ownership of corporations will gradually become apparent to executives and that something will be done about it. I believe also that the chances are good that business will develop its fair share of important thinkers.

My greatest doubts relate to the abiliy of business to win the friendship and confidence of the community — to develop a large number of executives who are so broad in their interests and so deeply concerned with the problems of the non-business parts of the community that the community is friendly toward business and that the spokesmen of business win a good hearing. This represents the crux of the problem. If business can convince the community that business leaders wish to help find solutions for community problems, the important thinkers in the business world will be able to win acceptance for a fair share of their ideas.

The community will, of course, remain in the main a laboristic one, but business will recover part of the intellectual initiative which it has lost in the last generation. As a result, the community, which is now in danger of being transformed into one in which business has an insignificant voice, will become a genuinely coöperative one. Both labor and management will help mold policy, the important thinkers in the business world will win acceptance for a fair share of their ideas, and business will succeed in making its proper contribution to determining the course of history.

## THE CHALLENGE FOR LEADERSHIP IN A WELFARE ECONOMY

BY

*Thomas G. Spates*

VICE-PRESIDENT, PERSONNEL ADMINISTRATION

GENERAL FOODS CORPORATION

NEW YORK, NEW YORK

Every business leader today must cope with the impact of the trend toward the Welfare State. He knows the trend is bad for business and bad for the employees, leading inevitably to a loss of freedom and opportunity for the individual.

But what can the business leader do about this trend? What, if anything, can he do in his own company to keep employees from following the "something for nothing" philosophy?

Mr. Spates comes squarely to grips with these perplexing problems. He advocates that all companies adopt a concrete program which he calls "The American Code of Personnel Administration." This Code sets forth sixteen points that any business can follow, and Mr. Spates makes an eloquent and convincing appeal in their behalf. He concludes by urging the organization of "business task forces" to carry the program to all companies.

Mr. Spates is qualified by background and accomplishments to give advice on solutions to the difficult problems of people at the places where they work.

He assumed his present position more than thirteen years ago, after broad experience in the United States and Europe as a consultant on personnel administration and labor relations. He has contributed importantly to the present progressive position of General Foods in the field of personnel administration. For his outstanding work he received the first Award of Merit given by the New York Personnel Management Association in 1948.

## THE CHALLENGE FOR LEADERSHIP IN A WELFARE ECONOMY

A fundamental challenge to business leadership is found in a powerful and potentially convincing set of circumstances, of imperative concern to our national life.

First in this set of circumstances is the constant and merciless pressure of totalitarian communism. Second is the continued emphasis, by political leaders, of the people's dependence on the generosity of a strong central government. Third is the advocacy of a further extension of socialistic collectivism by a few, but highly influential, leaders of organized labor.

The impact and the implications of this set of vital circumstances demand the most serious scrutiny, analysis, and action by those who have any claim to business leadership, and certainly by those of us who serve as advisers for personnel administration.

### THE GREAT AMERICAN DREAM

Let's start this scrutiny and analysis by trying to see the entire United States of America in one look. It is quite an experience. Although we are inclined to take it for granted, it is really something amazing and stupendous.

Here in this land of ours, from the Atlantic to the Pacific, are all the differences and diversities of race, religion, politics, economics, and geography that are given as the reasons why the countries of western Europe have never been able to unite. And yet, instead of flying apart into several nationalistic pieces, we have held together through wars and peace, and have gained in united strength, power, and prestige.

The panorama may have at times seemed bewildering and confusing, but the explanation of this greatest of all human achievements is fairly simple.

As the people who settled and developed this country reached its shores, they celebrated their individual independence from oppression and autocratic domination in every form. They were bound together by a passionate love for freedom and opportunity. That *used to be* "the promise of America" — the great American dream. It was the mightiest of all dreams even though disturbed by an occasional nightmare.

Among the nightmares that have disturbed the American dream are the bloody conflicts that marked the spread of the industrial revolution across the United States. These conflicts were between leaders who wanted to be free to exploit human resources as well as physical resources, and men who revolted against unilateral repeal of their rights as human beings.

When the government entered these conflicts as a sort of referee, it was usually on the side of the leaders of business who were firmly in the driver's seat during the early decades of industrialization.

Also early in the twentieth century there emerged a few business leaders who believed and demonstrated that it was profitable as well as humane to treat their employees like human beings. Their results were sufficiently impressive to arouse interest and even envy abroad. Some countries of western Europe and Australia sent missions here to investigate. But most business leaders continued either to ignore or to ridicule the enlightened example set by the few.

### OBSCURING THE AMERICAN DREAM

Then came the great depression. At that point in our national history the leaders of government took over the driver's seat. They might have made an objective analysis of cause and effect, taken a long-range view, and instituted some necessary but balanced reforms. They might have led a crusade for renewed faith in basic moral concepts. They might have licked the depression without sacrificing the philosophy and the principles upon which this nation was founded and became great in spite of the weaknesses of man.

Instead, they chose forcefully and unceremoniously to heave business leaders generally into the far corners of the dog house. They chose to import some philosophies and methods of doubtful merit in the long-range interests of all the people, used by countries from which their ancestors had fled. And they let a new set of leaders occupy the driver's seat. Many of these leaders proceeded to abuse their newly acquired power, disregard the public interest, and draw upon their own heads the condemnation of the American people.

For a while it seemed as though a reasonable balance was being struck between major contending and sometimes conflicting interests. But a series of disillusioning events following the November election of 1948 have revealed a renewal of the political alliance between labor leaders and the federal administration. There has been a rededication to the policy of achieving the more abundant life through more taxes, more spending, more controls, and less liberty, and a clear declaration that government should stand for the welfare of the people.

This declaration is a far cry from the American idea of government as the servant of the people and a guarantor of equality of opportunity. Under the further implementation of this declaration the people will grow weaker and the government stronger, as demonstrated by the extent to which the American people have already succumbed to the anesthesia of federalized benevolent statism.

### LABOR LEADERS MOVE INTO THE ACT

Not to be outdone by the government, some leaders of organized labor have moved again into the center of the act. This time they offer a program for "coördinated Democratic industrial planning," which is supposed to be some place between American capitalism and European socialism. To one impartial observer the proposal looks "about as revolutionary as ever has been seriously made to change the relationship of the owners, managers and workers of industry."

To some of us who were associated with the Office of Production Management during the war this program appears to be a revival of the effort — then seriously made by a prominent labor leader — to restrict the freedom, authority, and effectiveness of executive decisions in all functions of general management — not only in personnel administration.

But that isn't all. Other leaders of organized labor have entered the field for bigger and better benefits, preferably on an industry-wide basis. They want workers to feel a greater degree of dependence on the union for their welfare.

So, in the year 1949, we find big government which distributes pay checks to 14,000,000 people, and big labor, with its 15,000,000 members, competing with each other as benefactors of the American people. In this competition they vie with each other in distributing a variety of packages, enticingly wrapped and labeled "Security." But these packages contain a time bomb that will blow up in our faces, provided we are still strong enough to be holding the package when the explosion occurs.

### THE OPPORTUNITY FOR BUSINESS LEADERS

Now it seems to me that the stage is all set and it is high time for the business leaders of the United States to get back into the act and enter this competition in a big way for the greatest of all stakes. Does anyone think that I am about to advocate entering this competition for leadership in a welfare economy by striving to outbid the two other major competitors in promising to provide bigger and better material values? If so, perish the thought. Quite the contrary. I want them to lead off from a foundation of imperishable fundamentals of the human spirit.

For half a generation now, leaders of government and leaders of organized labor have been appealing to the weaknesses in man — fear, greed, laziness, and self-pity. I want the leaders of business to base their platform on an appeal to the strengths in man — courage, enterprise, industriousness, and self-respect.

I want the leaders of business, individually and through their numerous associations across the country, to enter this competition — ***not against*** the government, ***not against*** organized labor — but *for* the proposition that every one of the millions of people on their payrolls is entitled to be treated like a human being.

That's quite a proposition. But at this stage in the competition there is no use even trying to settle for less.

Just what am I driving at? Shall I be more explicit? Well, I'll try — by challenging American business leaders to proclaim their support of this proposition, to make it their major project for 1949–50. They can show their support tangibly by organizing a task force of one hundred top executives who will tour the country urging their fellow executives and their associations to give unrestricted priority for the next twelve months to the ways of treating the people on their payrolls as individuals. For treatment as individuals is one of the surest ways to convince people that freedom and opportunity are worth fighting for, even if they have to tighten their belts while riding out an economic storm.

In these times, neither skepticism, tradition, nor lack of precedent should stand in the way of putting the vitality of outstanding business leaders back of this proposition and its implementation.

GUIDE FOR THE TASK FORCE

How is it done? And what are the chances of success in terms of the long-range interests of all the people and the survival of this nation as a democracy? Well, the time is short, but there's still a fighting chance.

At the disposal of business leaders, for use in this intense and dramatic competition, is the American Code of Personnel Administration. This code has stood the tests of troublous times and varied conditions. It stands today as the last bulwark of defense anywhere against socialistic collectivism and totalitarian communism.

Time does not permit elaboration of the contents of this code. But here is an outline of its sixteen major guide lines:

1. In all phases of the business practice high standards of character and morality. Thus the institution will stand as a source of inspiration which endows all other personal practices with qualities of honesty and integrity. This practice helps everyone on the payroll keep his chin up even when the going gets tough.

2. Provide everyone on the payroll with a written statement of principles of personal administration, consistent with the philosophy upon which our nation was founded, and act on those principles courageously in every situation.

3. Supply leadership which is motivated by high standards of administration rather than by expediency and exploitation. There are volumes of testimony and some scientific data to support the conclusion that the greatest single factor in the productivity of the individual is his mental attitude toward his boss.

4. Establish an organization concept and structure which follows sound principles affecting authority, responsibility, planning, coördination, control, and channels of communication. Developing a personnel program without a sound organization structure is like putting frosting on a poor piece of cake.

5. Designate a well-qualified person in the highest level of general management who will specialize in solving the problems of people and seeing to it that the code is made effective. This person should be selected according to the same standards of personal and technical competence used for other important members of general management.

6. Practice satisfying the desire for participation, by means of consultation and explanation, both up and down, through all echelons of organization. If one were forced, under pain of severe punishment, to express the essence of sound personnel administration in just two words, those words would be "Consultation" and "Explanation."

7. Keep everyone on the payroll informed on all matters affecting his interests.

8. Encourage freedom of expression of points of view and attitudes, without fear of reprisals.

9. Create a total work environment that appeals to the self-respect and dignity of the individual.

10. Make certain that everyone is given a sympathetic consideration of his trials and tribulations, particularly supervisors who too often are not given time or the opportunity to air their gripes.

11. Try to provide steady, certain employment. It is the psychological rather than the financial aspect of this practice that justifies its inclusion here.

12. Develop a program of promotional opportunity. Mere statement of a policy of promotion from within is not enough. People like to have answers to the questions "Where do I go from here?" and "By what route?"

13. Establish equitable wage and salary structures that recognize differences in job and position requirements, as measured by such factors as knowledge, skill, difficulty, and responsibility.

14. Develop a training program designed to help everyone perform his tasks in the best known ways.

15. Provide for recognition of the individual, particularly through personal evaluation, so that it may be said to each person on the payroll, "He is prepared with what to go where" — and "he knows the score."

16. Diffuse a spirit of friendliness throughout the business. Friendliness, the essence of all good human relations, should play upon people like the sunlight that pierces the clouds or casts a pattern of light and shade through the woods in the autumn.

Are you aware that there is no reference in this code either to absolute wages or benefit plans? The reason is this. Not only does the source of sound personnel administration reside in the conscience of leaders, but it is concerned primarily with the spirit and hearts of people. Those are qualitative factors. History offers no evidence that quantitative methods and rewards have ever provided the solution to qualitative problems.

### THE CODE WORKS

This code is simple. It is inexpensive in all but time and perseverance. And it works.

This code is being used with amazingly satisfactory results by many progressive and highly successful companies. In fact, among the companies using it are those with long, unbroken records of dividend payments. These users are having the minimum of difficulty in recruiting and retaining high quality personnel at all levels. They have the best reputations in the field of human relations. They have the longest and best records of industrial peace.

Why so much confidence in the results to be achieved in "the competition for leadership in a welfare economy" by the conscientious application of this code? Because it reduces the cost of managing a business. Because there is no satisfactory substitute. Because it is so universally acceptable that no one *dares* oppose it. Because the record still supports the conclusion that Americans prefer the American Code of Personnel Administration to unionism.

In the face of these impelling and irrefutable reasons, it becomes each day increasingly incomprehensible that so many executive leaders still fail to apply their leadership to achieving these goals in the field of human relations.

### GOOD PERSONAL ADMINISTRATION AND UNIONISM

Here are some old and new excerpts from the record which support the conclusion that Americans prefer good personnel administration to unionism:

From Hollywood in the 1930's:

> The directors, however, retained their old habits of revising manuscripts and, despite the fact that many of the writers were very able, continued to treat the authors as though they were hacks.

The free lance actors contributed their time and money to the guild because they felt that through it they gained dignity and independence. They had rebelled against the paternalism of the Academy.

From an AFL leader in San Francisco in March 1940:

I think I have said at both of the previous meetings that I have attended here at Stanford that there would be no need for labor unions if there were no dissatisfied workers; that dissatisfaction among employees is the germ which creates labor organizations. I said then and I repeat again, that if employers as a whole treated their employees half as well as they want the public to believe they treat them, we would have a fearful job organizing employees into trade unions.

In January 1941, from a fine, young AFL business agent who helped organize a General Foods plant on the west coast:

If there had been good industrial relations in your plant, I do not think the employes would have joined ours or any union.

Early in 1942 from the organizers of the Steel Workers Union:

One of the compelling motives for union membership is the desire of workers to give their personalities dignity and their lives a meaning. They join unions to become something more than a check number. They crave to be recognized as human beings. The dynamic quality, the militancy and the crusading spirit of the labor movement, especially of CIO in the last decade, were nurtured by the failure of management to satisfy the *non*-economic needs of the workers.

From a steel city in Pennsylvania in April 1947:

Management hasn't got enough understanding of working people and their problems. Businessmen keep thinking of labor as a commodity instead of human beings. The reason people join unions is because they feel that the boss won't pay any real attention to the welfare of the workers if left to himself. He's got to be forced to do things.

From a small town in the midwest, July 1947:

Our chief engineer was for some years business agent for the engineers' union in Omaha. He said if management would pursue modern personnel policies, most of the strife between industry and labor would never occur.

In January 1948, from a union officer in New England:

It was the memory of past abuses and the constantly fostered fear that the employers would seize upon even the slightest opportunity to force laboring men back to filthy shops and starvation wages which was the great uniting and driving force of the militant XYZ union.

In March 1948, from a CIO leader on the Pacific waterfront:

Do we develop, agitate, educate or propagandize our men to be more loyal to the union than to the employer? You bet we do. No matter what happens in these proceedings we will never do otherwise. It is our union policy and an official policy — that they can't trust an employer; that if they depend upon an employer for any type of security or fair treatment, they'll get stung. And that is what we tell them; that their security comes through the union; and that their living comes through the union.

From a small industrial town in New Jersey, May 1948:

The union believed that the company's pre-unionization paternalism still existed to some extent. The comprehensive personnel program created a fear in the minds of the union leaders that the net effect of the program would be to reduce the employes' interest in and *loyalty* to the union.

Developing a sense of solidarity would probably remain the principal concern of local union leaders. But they recognize that the workers' chief interests are in his personal and job situations.

In July 1948, from the editor of the CIO News:

Workers do not form unions for the sake of having organizations that they can call their own. They form unions because they have learned, often through bitter experience, that they must pool their energies and act collectively if they are to achieve satisfactory or near-satisfactory solutions to their problems in human relations which so often plague them.

From a Pulitzer prize-winning series of articles — "The New York Waterfront" — as recently reported in the *New York Sun:*

Five hundred men fought one another like animals for a hundred brass checks and a half day's work. That's your shape-up in New York, the greatest port in the world, and this is the twentieth century. It is difficult to get from the New York

Shipping Association, representing the employers, any real information about work practices and general conditions on the docks. They are reluctant to talk.

Again, back in Hollywood in December 1948, from a high-salaried movie star:

> In the future I shall gladly work for less if by so doing I can retain my claim upon the common decencies without which the most glorified job becomes intolerable, but with which the most humble can be carried out with dignity.

These and countless other excerpts from the record keep telling us over and over again that in the hearts of American workers, unionism is second best.

Despite this compelling testimony in support of the American Code of Personnel Administration, there is disconcerting evidence of the possibility that business leaders may lose this competition by default.

Now, let's make a couple of important items unmistakably clear. First, sound personnel administration is neither advocated nor practiced for the purpose of thwarting the growth of unionism. Second, there is not the slightest degree of incompatibility between sound personnel administration and collective bargaining through the chosen representatives of employees.

Quite the contrary. The record shows clearly that collective action helps to achieve and maintain many of the objectives of sound personnel administration. Far from detracting from the magnitude and importance of the personnel function, the process of collective action adds to both by revealing defects in organization and administration, and increasing the incentives for constructive action.

Also, let's be reminded that everyone on the payroll, from the chairman to the charwoman, is entitled to be treated like a human being. The American Code of Personnel Administration is designed to serve that end. There are a lot of people on the payroll who are not represented through collective bargaining.

When employees do decide to deal with management through their chosen representatives, it is the essence of good leadership to accept the decision graciously. It should be recognized that something new and different has been added to the normal methods of administration. With the help and advice of the employee representatives, your efforts to foster better employment relations should be intensified.

By pursuing that course with patience and perseverance you may expect, in time, to achieve the mutually satisfying results revealed in the following excerpts from a letter of January 17, 1949, received by one of our General Foods managers from the union negotiating committee:

> As the time for renewing our contract approaches we take this opportunity to acquaint you with a few items we would like to discuss. But first, let us express our thanks to the Company for the generous gesture made when, with no request from us, they raised our wages at the time the new job evaluation scheme was put into effect. The knowledge that this could have been withheld until our contract was renegotiated helped to strengthen still further the mutual goodwill and understanding which we have so long enjoyed.
>
> So, at this time, with the markets levelling off we are making no wage claims and feel sure that, should our optimism regarding prices be unfounded, you will, as in past years, be ready

to discuss it with us . . . That covers all we have in mind at this time and we trust that our negotiations will be carried through in the same spirit of harmony and goodwill that has prevailed in all our previous meetings.

SUCCESS REQUIRES ACTION AT THE WORK PLACE

The experiences of many companies provide similar and more spectacular demonstrations to prove beyond the shadow of a doubt that, through the conscientious use of the American Code of Personnel Administration, you can't lose. But, mark you well, there are no short cuts.

Seeing to it that people on the payroll are treated like human beings *at the places where they work* calls for the highest qualities of executive leadership, administrative intelligence, and eternal vigilance. Broadcasting the virtues of the American way of life through loud-speakers and billboards is futile. As a means of competing for leadership in a welfare economy, it is as hopeless as fighting a conflagration with a garden hose.

No — if the leaders of business are going to enter this competition for the greatest stakes in history, they must demonstrate *by daily deeds at the places where people work,* their belief in the philosophy and principles of the Declaration of Independence and the Bill of Rights. Through those sacred instruments and their implementation we established a land of freedom.

REFILLING FREEDOM'S RESERVOIRS

To anyone willing to grit his teeth and look reality squarely in the eye, it should be crystal clear by now that for the past decade our country has been getting by on the momentum of freedom we inherited. Refilling the reservoirs of freedom is the supreme and critical issue of our time. For in population, size, resources, leadership, and passion for industrialization, the United States of America has finally met its match in the U.S.S.R.

Our decisive advantage in that competition is the power of freedom. The leaders of American business have within their control the opportunity to replenish that power. For in this country conversion to the doctrine of totalitarianism is made at the places where people work, as a result of the way they are treated by their bosses at all levels of human organization.

### THE FINAL TESTIMONY

Are there still among you some who doubt the validity of my findings? Well, I'll offer one more piece of supporting testimony.

This testimony comes from Ralph Chaplin, a native-born American who, as a youngster, dedicated his life to the class struggle. He was an artist, a poet, an editor, a migratory worker, an agitator, a socialist, a communist, one of the foremost leaders of the Industrial Workers of the World. For his beliefs in the class struggle he was beaten by the goon squads of employers, served four years in Leavenworth, and faced union goon squads on the Pacific waterfront.

At the end of that trail, Mr. Chaplin, in his book entitled *Wobbly,* has this to ask and say:

> How were we to know that out of our "social revolution" would arise a new ruling class just as arrogant, just as merciless and just as predatory as its predecessor?

How were we to know that in the socialist millennium we were merely to exchange bosses and that our "emancipation" would mean, not the end of the exploitation of man by man, but the beginning of exploitation of man by the state?

How were we to know in 1918 that the glow in the eastern skies which so many of us greeted as the Red Dawn was in reality the funeral pyre of freedom?

Some one smarter than I [says Chaplin], will have to come up with the ultimate answers. But what I have in mind is a revitalized American ideology, one that would enable the Sermon on the Mount and the Bill of Rights to do more than hold their own in competition with Das Kapital and the Communist Manifesto. It would make our America physically, ideologically and morally the most dynamic of all nations.

On these findings and this testimony I now rest the case for my basic proposition. Business leaders of the past and present have made great and enduring contributions to the welfare and glory of this nation. They have never yet failed the American people in a national emergency. In the current competition for leadership in a welfare economy the most powerful weapon of business leaders is the proposition that everyone on their payrolls is entitled to be treated like a human being. Through vigorous and courageous use of this weapon, they have it within their power to refill the reservoirs of freedom and so to help preserve our inalienable rights to life, liberty, and the pursuit of happiness.

God grant that our business leaders may arise to this supreme emergency and be truly worthy of their hire— so that it may be inscribed of them in the great book that this was "their finest hour."

## THE BUSINESS LEADER'S LARGER JOB

BY

*L. R. Boulware*

VICE-PRESIDENT, EMPLOYEE RELATIONS

GENERAL ELECTRIC COMPANY

NEW YORK, NEW YORK

In his section, Dr. Slichter showed why businessmen have lost the position of leadership and prestige they once enjoyed. Then Mr. Spates developed a concrete program for regaining lost ground through positive executive action within the business.

In this section, Mr. Boulware moves the business leader to the arena outside his business. He points out the peril that business is in and shows the businessman specifically how to put on an attack that will regain lost ground and, in so doing, serve the public interest.

The words "arena" and "attack" are used advisedly. For Mr. Boulware comes out fighting. Clearly he is aroused by what he sees going on. And he pounds home a powerful message, which includes a step-by-step program for getting employees and the general public to recognize that a favorable climate for business is important to them.

A graduate of the University of Wisconsin, where he was captain of the baseball team, Mr. Boulware later became a captain of infantry in World War I. After experience as a teacher, public accountant, comptroller, and factory manager, Mr. Boulware was general sales manager of Easy Washing Machine Company for ten years. Then he was successively general manager of Carrier Corporation and Celotex Corporation.

During World War II Mr. Boulware was Operations Vice-Chairman of the War Production Board. For outstanding work in this position he received the Medal of Merit.

After the war, Mr. Boulware became general manager of General Electric's manufacturing subsidiaries. Then in a surprise move in June 1947, he was charged with responsibility for carrying out a new concept of Charles E. Wilson, president of General Electric. General Electric has determined to be as successful in bringing out improved model jobs and selling them to employees as it has been in bringing out improved model products and selling them to customers.

Mr. Boulware is currently busy putting into effect the program he outlines in this section. He has accepted many invitations to speak, has appeared before Senate committees, and has become a fighting advocate of "what's good for business is good for the public."

I suspect that you are humbled — as are most businessmen — by a growing sense of failure right in the midst of success.

THE BUSINESSMAN'S PARADOX

We are great physicists, chemists, engineers. We are phenomenal manufacturers. We have been fabulous financiers. We are superb at individual selling and mass marketing.

Yet as the *whole man* of business — the manager and leader — we are condemned. When we try to merchandise the over-all economic and social consequences of our operations, we fail. In fact, it has become the habit of politicians to believe that the way to *sure* election is to promise to correct the businessman's wicked abuses of employees and of the public. This is a successful habit not just of cheap and ill-mannered politicians, but of those of the most impeccable backgrounds of family and education.

People like — and respect — the results of our separate professional skills. But taken as a whole, our activities are too likely to be regarded as antisocial by a majority of the public.

Mr. Joseph A. Lee, Vice-President of Standard Brands, Inc., said recently, "The people will go into the stores and vote for your products by purchasing them, and then go to the polls and vote you out of business."

Our situation is like that of the Taft-Hartley law. People — and union members — like each separate provision of the law but have been taught to question the law as a whole. Yet we businessmen are people of the highest ability and the best intentions; we are the architects of the highest standard of living in history, both for material and spiritual well-being.

How do we find ourselves in this situation? Our customers, stockholders, and vendors approve of us, to be sure. But our employees, the unions, the government, too often the educators and clergy, too much of the public — in other words our real bosses — do not respect or like us, or even appreciate or understand us. In fact, they do not even credit us with good intentions — with being on their side. However, we thoroughly believe that being on their side is being on the side of what's good for all.

People just don't think that the jobs we businessmen provide are what they ought to be. They don't think that the economic and social consequences of our activities, and the system back of our activities, are what they ought to be for the good of each community and of the nation. They think that we are smart, skilled, technically honest, but coldly selfish and not on the side of employees and the public.

As a result, they not only do not *seek* our participation in important affairs, in the running of the country — they openly oppose it. We are invariably ruled out of all councils as undesirables. Yet we are the same people who give largely those same people the products, prices, jobs, and investments they like in the individual cases.

WHAT CAN BE DONE?

What can be the matter? Whose fault is it? What ought to be done? And who ought to do this undone task, the business leader's larger job? I am presuming these are questions that are being asked by everyone who is a business leader or aspires to business leadership.

At General Electric, where we have all these questions, we decided two years ago that we, at least, would try to do something about this businessman's paradox. We concluded that we must come to grips with these puzzling problems. We determined not to go on about our customary pursuits, being technically successful there, while appearing to be failing in the larger and the only really important sphere of true personal accomplishment and real social usefulness. We, like too many others, were winning the skirmishes as before, but these successses seemed to be having less and less influence on winning important battles, much less the war.

We decided to draw on our successful sales and general management experience in determining how to do a better job of employee and community relations. First, we used typical market research to learn the likes and dislikes of our employees. Then, using product planning methods, we concluded that all of us in management — including each foreman — should work toward giving each employee a new-model job which would have nine specific features the employees had said they wanted.

APPROACHING THE NEW MODEL JOB

We approached the nine-point, new-model job on three fronts:

1. We decided to get and keep pay, working conditions, and other material characteristics of each job up to the ever-rising standards — and to do this *voluntarily*.

But we found — as everyone does — that these material things are not enough. Although the employee is showered with riches and works in a palace, that never satisfies his quest for significance or meets his other requirements for job satisfaction. He doesn't live by bread alone.

2. So next we set about training supervisors at all levels to established genuine, continuous, and intimate two-way communication with each employee. We try to get each supervisor to treat each employee as an individual — to respect his dignity, supply him with desired information, and give him a real sense of importance and participation. In short, we try to get our supervisors to act like salesmen instead of bosses so that the employee has the desire to do what's wanted and does not have to be driven to do it.

I am passing over these two points hurriedly because they have been ably discussed previously by that wise and successful practitioner of what he preaches — Thomas G. Spates. I want to spend my time on a third area of neglect and need that we think we have located for the business leader who is interested in doing his larger job.

3. We think we have found that it is not enough for the employee — or his family and neighbors — to feel he has got the best pay, best working conditions, and best

boss in town. Nor is it enough if he feels his boss and company are on his side and are really putting human considerations first. We feel the employee must also understand simple economics — something about how our system works.

For example, the employee goes into the grocery store and finds prices that seem outlandishly high. Remembering the warnings of the politicians, he concludes that the system back of his boss — and of which his boss, the grocer, and all businessmen are the representatives — is not being operated by people on his side but by people who are against him, by people who may be exploiting him. Unfortunately, economic facts will not speak for themselves any more than product and sales facts. They have got to be constantly pointed out and explained to the public just as product and sales facts do to customers.

### NEED FOR ECONOMIC UNDERSTANDING

And right here we run into what I think is the most pressing problem of our times: getting a better understanding of economics. We know, for instance, how to price our jobs. We know how to sell our job "customers" on the human factors. But in the field of economic literacy we need desperately to transfer to that area the skills we have developed so fully in marketing our products.

But in this third area we have virtually no skills. For example, few of us know, or can put convincingly in words of one syllable, the reasons why our profits are not the cause of high prices as the left-wingers charge. Even at the top too few of us really know our economics — the relation of wages, prices, taxes, and profits; the function of savings and of investment in technological advances; the social gains of incentives and competition in a free market of millions of individual decisions versus central planning; how we have raised and can raise our real wages, our real standard of living; how we get into a disinflation like the present; and how we can get soundly through it and come out into a healthy period instead of another silly and debilitating spree.

Why is it so frightening for businessmen, for employees, for all serious and patriotic citizens not to know — and not to be teaching and discussing — sound economics and sensible political conduct? It's because of the new kind of robber barons that have gotten more and more successful elsewhere around the world during the last thirty years. They always first get themselves outwardly cloaked in the mantle of the common man. But their objective is power — direct power rather than power through money. Therefore, their methods are political and not commercial.

Meanwhile in country after country businessmen have been gradually weakened and then displaced because they unthinkingly continued to devote themselves solely to their customary commercial pursuits, where their only skill is. Along with their displacement went freedom for all the people — freedom and any hope of human dignity, plenty, and the good life.

After seeing this at work abroad among our enemies and our allies alike for thirty years, what do we find ourselves doing? How are we Americans acting, we who are so well off that even our so-called "ill-fed, ill-housed, and ill-clothed lower third" is the envy of the rest of the world? How are natively smart Americans acting, we who not only have finest basic educations but have had experience of others enacted right before us so that we don't have to theorize, experiment, or take any foolish chances?

How are we acting? Just as though we have been studying up to be half-wits!

First, we are putting on a great spectacle of how sorry we are for ourselves. Our plight seems tragic indeed! Last year we only treated ourselves to one million new homes, four and one-half million refrigerators, and almost five million motor vehicles in addition to about 38 million already on wheels at the beginning of the year. And right now, with the possibility of some overdue readjustment looking us in the face, we still seem to be making progress toward going out and getting in each other's way with an additional four to five million cars this year.

We must remember that right now, when the faces of management, labor, and government are showing a little anxiety, we still have the purchasing power required for good times. Ninety-four per cent of the work force is still employed at high pay. And these people are still saving at a more rapid rate every week, as the statements of the saving banks indicate. People have bought what they wanted most and were willing to pay too much for. They still need and want millions of the same and other things. But most of them are holding on to old savings and putting more away in the bank. People are getting along with things they have while waiting for more attractive products and prices.

We have to admit we live in a fantastic fairyland of well-being when we consider the new burdens we are carrying and when we contrast our well-being with that of any other country in the world, now or at any other time. But people are being taught to look right at these facts and not see them.

Second, we bought all these new things and made all these savings after handing over taxes to our federal government at a rate of over 40 billion dollars a year. And get this picture! Half of this 40 billion dollars of taxes is being spent to ward off the foreign collectivist menace to our system and our safety. But right at the same time too many of us here at home — in and out of government, unions, and business — are joyously, if not hysterically, embracing one after another of the very ideas, influences, features, or ingredients of this same collectivism that can surely lead us into the exact type of police state we so fear — the very police state of poverty, slavery, and hopelessness that we are fighting with our billions.

### CAUSES OF LOSS OF BUSINESS INFLUENCE

How do people all over the world get this way? Why do they reject businessmen, who have a fine record of raising the standard of living through voluntary action inspired by the incentive to save and to compete? Why do so many choose, instead, the government planners? To be sure, these planners promise security and plenty. But history shows they skim off for state purposes everything above a bare subsistence standard of living. And even their recent record clearly shows the inevitable necessity in the end of directly or indirectly shutting off free speech in order that their planning failures will be masked.

People all over the world have acted that way — and still do — for two reasons. First, pitifully few businessmen have had the alertness to know when they have been pushed beyond the commercial field into the political arena. Second, even when they have awakened to the facts, too few businessmen have seemingly had the courage, intelligence, or energy to go about correcting misinformation and teaching sound economics. Yet they would have no trouble or the slightest hesitancy in dealing devastatingly in the commercial field with essentially the exact type of spurious emotional attacks and something-for-nothing appeals.

We businessmen are bold and imaginative before business competitors. We are cowardly and dumb in public when confronted with union and other political doctrines contrary to our beliefs and interests.

WHAT SHOULD BUSINESSMEN DO?

What, then, do we have to do to be saved? It seems to me that all we have to do is exactly what we do when we encounter any other unsound or unfair salesman trying to compete for our customer's favor. We take a good look at our product, make certain again that it's right in function and price for the current market, and then sell the daylights right out of the something-for-nothing boys. In fact, I'll bet all of you honorable and experienced executives hope for no greater blessing than that your competitors will show up as liars and with bad products. To a good salesman with an honest product, it's like shooting fish in a barrel from there on, and you know it.

A distinguished M.I.T. professor told me recently that he was beginning to believe that the missing ingredient in employee relations, community relations, and public relations was summed up in the one word "politics." By that he meant political activity by managers, stockholders, bondholders, insurance policyholders, savings bank depositors, pensioners, and others with an interest in keeping the value of money honest, the standard of living rising, and the freedom of choice, speech, and movement really free.

I would agree if by "political activity" he meant the mastery of sound economics and the insistence by citizens on sound economic teaching and sound economic practices by their representatives in government, in unions, even in education and the clergy, as well as in business.

Those who have been in Washington recently know that while there *is* a selling job to be done there, that is not the place for the primary selling job. Senators and Representatives are like furniture buyers sent to the annual market. They do not have much leeway for their own discretion or taste. They do—and are supposed to do—what the folks back home want done. If they have been sent to market to buy "borax" or "schlacht" goods, or think they have, there's no use trying to persuade them to follow their own taste in period furniture. They must get changed instructions from home. These changed instructions can come only as a result of correcting misinformation and sound reëducation back there at the grass roots.

I am so bold personally as to believe that right now a great majority in the present Senate and House are hoping they will not have to vote for several very specific projects that seem just around the corner. They are hoping for word from home, I think, which will indicate that the folks back there will understand if they, as legislators, do right and refuse the pressures of highly organized and active minorities to do what is unsound in the real public interest.

There is a great big test going on now, it seems to me, to determine if there really is a mandate for this whole package or if, in fact, there is a mandate for any single one among this group of projects that I feel are loaded with such disastrous possibilities. This test is in connection with the efforts at labor law revision.

For example, I sincerely believe that a majority of the present Senate and House would like to keep the Taft-Hartley law pretty much as is — especially its most important provisions covering the closed shop, jurisdictional disputes, injunctions, secondary boycotts, featherbedding, communism in unions, responsibility of unions to live up to their contracts, accountability of union officers to members, and freedom from bargaining with foremen's unions so likely to become dominated by workers' unions. I'm sure a majority does not favor plant seizure and submission of an employer's intimate financial data to what may be a hostile Department of Labor.

But under the influence of presumed or claimed mandates, and under the pressure of a tightly organized and unbelievably zealous minority, we have seen Republicans appear to be joining the Democrats and Democrats appear to be joining the Republicans, all acting outwardly as though they were frantically fleeing from something. Right from the start of this Congress, sobering news from home indicated that the wishes of the folks back there were being misinterpreted.

This flood of news supporting most all the present provisions of Taft-Hartley grew to a clamor — quite contrary to what a lot of people had planned. But developments of the last couple of months can only indicate that the people's battle for a law that's fair to the public, to employees, and to employers, is by no means won. It is still in grave danger of being lost.

Businessmen, and an unusual number of other leaders and individual citizens, got busy early this year and expressed themselves convincingly to their Congressmen and Senators. This resulted in the defeat of the forces seeking a return to the old Wagner Act with its abuses of employees, employers, and public. But the defeat was only temporary. While businessmen and other citizens have been returning to their usual productive pursuits, a combination of union and administrative forces have been working day and night to apply to Representatives and Senators every pressure that can possibly be produced by zeal and by patronage and other tremendous, politically usable funds. Businessmen and other fair-minded citizens must return to this battle. They must put it ahead of usual commercial pursuits. And there will be more causes like this one that must have the same support.

### INDIVIDUAL ACTIVITY IN THE PUBLIC INTEREST

Who is to do something about all these things? In the critical days ahead, who is to keep on talking to his Congressmen and friends about labor laws that are in the public interest? Who is to learn and then teach economics? Who is to put his citizenship duties ahead of his commercial duties?

I can't speak for others. But I can tell you it is my conviction, and the conviction of member after member of our General Electric management force of 15,000, not to look to others or to try to delegate this job of good citizenship to subordinates or to associations. We are going to try to do our part of this job ourselves — each of us to the degree we can attain the personal facility and command the interest of others in the things we are trying to do in the public interest. For we have become acutely aware that the public interest is now the individual selfish interest of each of us. And it isn't just enlightened self-interest. It's self-preservation, the first law of nature.

We have seen — and are seeing — our Representatives and Senators. We have testified before House and Senate committees. We are telling our neighbors back at the grass roots what we think. We are learning economics and teaching economics to our supervisors, our 200,000 employees, and seven million neighbors in our plant cities. We are discussing in public print every controversial public issue that involves job connected economics or the effect of public policy on us, our employees, or our neighbors.

To be sure, many capable businessmen question whether we are being wise or prudent. But to us nothing is going to matter if, through failure even to try to seek the truth and to speak up publicly in discussing it, our country should go the way of others — in ignorance and cowardice — to end our freedom, hope, and material and spiritual well-being.

For my money — as an individual — I think it is the job of every individual citizen in and out of business to speak up in the public interest. But I believe the greatest obligation is imposed on him who has the greatest opportunity. And there can be no question but that the businessman has the greatest opportunity. He has the pick of the people with courage and skills. He has the money. The channels of communication are still open to his use. In his organization, selling, and advertising work he is already the great mass and individual student and teacher.

THE BUSINESSMAN'S PROGRAM

Here is what I think we as businessmen ought to do to contribute to the understanding, preservation, and improvement of our free and wonderfully productive system of incentives and competition:

1. Before anything else, we have got to be born again. We must shake a lifetime's habit of mind about values. We must undergo a real inner regeneration that gives us a moving conviction about the necessity, the profit, and the pleasure of putting human considerations first. We have got to develop new habits of two-way communication, association, and participation with our employees at all levels. And we must like all this.

We have got to realize that to keep from failing as commercial leaders from here on, we must first become deserving of success as human leaders, as Americans if you will, as businessmen and citizens doing our larger job. From here on sound political accomplishment in the true sense is a requirement for any continued commercial success of the type we seek — continued improvement in our standard of physical living and spiritual well-being.

2. Of course, we must continue to provide good jobs and good bosses. And we must make these benefits known to

our employees, to their neighbors, and to the public—just as we have made all these people recognize that we make good products. We can do this in the job field if we will do exactly what we do in the product field both to deserve and to get favorable recognition.

3. Then we come to what's truly our larger job. That's the job of deserving and getting a favorable economic climate for our operations, and then deserving and getting favorable recognition for the over-all economic and social contributions of business.

I think the prescription for achieving these goals is very simple. The public merely needs to understand the rudiments of sound economics and then insist that its representatives in business, government, unions, and elsewhere be guided by the sound principles of economics so learned. Although the prescription is simple, *filling* the prescription is a difficult, tedious, and long task. To fill it requires a more or less complete change in our habit of letting economic literacy take care of itself. And unfortunately, this is a habit that usually is the more pronounced the higher up in management a given executive is.

But the job's got to be done if business management—in fact, if our free system—is to survive. I think it *can* be done if we will recognize and do something about the following:

(a) We in top management must not only *learn* sound economics but so *master* the subject that each of us is a competent teacher of it. Even beyond that, each of us must be an *example* of one who has a clear confidence in the soundness of his position. The businessman must be willing and able to mount the platform or face the radio microphone or television camera and argue rings around any advocate of collectivism or other something-for-nothing philosophies. In fact, he must seek opportunities to do so.

(b) Having qualified as teachers and examples ourselves, we must then go on to see that people in management, at all levels, become competent teachers of sound economics and inspiring examples of ready and convincing speakers, or even debaters, on the subject.

(c) Still *not* calling on somebody way off somewhere else to "do something about it" while we go about our customary pursuits, we must keep on right at home with our own employees and see that we prove we can explain to them, and inspire their confidence in, this free system of ours. This should include the relationships of wages, prices, taxes, profits, savings, technological improvements, capital formation, retained earnings, etc.

Who among you would volunteer now to mount a public platform and debate with a left-wing union or political leader on topics such as these: how we got into this recession; how to get out of it our way instead of his way; the functions of profits; whether profits are too high and are causing high prices and unemployment; why deficit financing is bad and what is the substitute for it; why higher wages now will not cure unemployment and what will? Not many would volunteer, I am sure.

We must *really know* what we are *for* as well as what we are *against*. We must be willing to volunteer to teach and to debate. We must be able to prevail over the unsound advocates who have been and are so busy in such great numbers and with such zeal. Until we can do those things, there is no real chance of having people stop believing misinformation and begin believing our way. One of the great tragedies of our time is that so many of us Americans in and out of management do not know what "our way" is.

(d) Once we have proved our competence within our own business organizations, we must then get out into the communities where we operate and try to help the families and neighbors of our employees begin to solve the economic and citizenship problems about which they are so puzzled, so troubled, so anxious. And we can't delay going beyond our factory and office walls.

We find the typical General Electric employee averages fifty neighbors. We have found it frustrating to give an employee correct economic information about something that is bothering him and then let him go home to face fifty neighbors who are not correctly informed on the subject and who therefore attack the things he has learned. Consequently, our economic and policy messages to our 200,000 employees are repeated as paid advertisements in the daily newspapers of our plant communities and reach almost seven million of our employees' neighbors.

(e) But the printed word and the other activities of any one employer are not enough. So, after developing the habit of doing his duty by his own employees and their families and neighbors to the extent he alone can reach them, then business leaders must try to interest others in similar activities or other activities with the same objective of sound economic education for all, looking toward sound commercial and citizenship practices.

Other employers in the same communities ought to be

persuaded to engage privately and publicly in adult economic education — to concentrate on, not avoid, controversial issues. Employers should seek to get sponsorship of economic study and discussion sessions by newspapers, radio and television stations, chambers of commerce, employers associations, churches and service clubs, groups of stockholders, bondholders, insurance policyholders, and savings bank depositors. These should not be one-shot affairs. They must be part of a way of life until we can get a clear understanding of how people do act — and how we all *ought* to act — in the face of material needs and material desires. For that is about all the study of economics is.

(f) One of the best starters, I believe, is the city-wide adult economics course. General Electric has been a party to some experiments where 400 to 700 businessmen, serious union leaders, and other leading citizens took a course of thirteen lessons in elementary economics. They paid ten dollars each. Yet there was never anything but standing room, so great was the interest.

This interest we find everywhere. It is simply up to us all, as leaders, to find the individual means for harnessing this interest toward establishing a body of sound economic information in the minds of a majority of the public.

I could go on, but I am sure you are already way ahead of me. The methods you develop will be better than these beginning suggestions of mine.

But let's do covenant together

— that *we ourselves* are going to understand this wonderful system of ours

—that we are going to find out how to preserve and improve it rather than let it be damaged or even perish

—that we are going to do our part in seeing that a majority of citizens understands the economic facts of life, the proper working of our system, and the fallacy of all these contrary something-for-nothing fairy tales

—that we are going to encourage an increasing majority of citizens to insist very vocally that their representatives in business, government, and unions act with economic horse-sense

—and that a few of us individuals are going to constitute ourselves as a brave and, if necessary, expendable force that is going to be the first to put these things really first in our daily business and personal lives.

Yes, let's be sure a great many of us covenant that we are going to assume leadership in the larger job of standing up, talking out, and being counted. Let's speak out for what our study and experience persuade us is best for the further attainment of the greatest material and spiritual needs and desires of the greatest number of people. Let's speak up, *no matter who has to be contradicted!*

PART II

# Steps in Developing
# The Kind of Business Leaders We Need

## EXPERIENCE IN THE DEVELOPMENT OF MANAGEMENT PEOPLE

BY

*William B. Given, Jr.*

PRESIDENT

AMERICAN BRAKE SHOE COMPANY

NEW YORK, NEW YORK

Stockholders and employees have a vital, mutual interest in the caliber of the executives managing their companies. For executive performance determines whether the stock is a "good buy" or the company "a good place to work." Usually the two go hand in hand.

Despite the obvious importance to everyone concerned of having capable managers, most companies let the development of executives "take care of itself." And the total number of companies with well-planned and effectively carried out executive development programs remains surprisingly small even after diligent efforts to discover them.

Top-management executives who are unhappy with this business paradox will find much concrete and specific help in Mr. Given's discussion of what his company is doing to develop management people.

Mr. Given is a product of the policy he preaches and practices — promotion from within the ranks. A graduate of Yale, he joined Brake Shoe in 1911 as secretary to the president. He climbed to presidential assistant in 1916 before leaving for World War I to serve as a lieutenant and then captain in the infantry.

Returning from the war, he became assistant vice-president in 1919, vice-president in 1921, and president in

1929. His philosophy of management has been more extensively set forth in his book, *Bottom-Up Management* (Harper and Brothers).

Mr. Given is a director of Bankers Trust Company; Mellon National Bank & Trust Company; Dry Dock Savings Bank; Combustion Engineering — Superheater, Inc.; and Bucyrus-Erie Company. His educational and charitable activities include directorates in the American Red Cross and Legal Aid Society of New York; trusteeships of General Theological Seminary and the Industrial Hygiene Foundation; and chairmanship of the Committee for University Development, Yale University.

## EXPERIENCE IN THE DEVELOPMENT OF MANAGEMENT PEOPLE

The future of any business depends more on the people in it than on any other single element. The success of any company compared with others in the industry depends largely on its ability to bring in and develop the right kind of men for management responsibilities.

### TEST OF TOP MANAGEMENT

Directors, and an increasing number of stockholders, are more critical today than ever before in their comments on companies which fail to develop their own executive material. They censure severely managements which frequently find it necessary to bring outsiders into important positions. It is now well recognized that the responsibility for such a situation within a company rests not on the company's chief executive but on the board of directors — if they retain the chief executive. Only men who develop their own management people qualify for this position.

To me the two most challenging business problems are developing management people within the company and building the intrinsic value of its equity securities. Success in the first builds greater success in the second.

An efficient staff, growing continually more effective, strengthens any company. Successful operation draws more good young people into the ranks and is a top incentive for them to remain. Each requires both concentration and patience.

There is no shortage of young men who can be developed into outstanding executives. There is, however, a shortage of men who *have* been developed. In a minor degree this is due to the fact that few young men were available for business training during the war period. In a major degree it is due to management's failure in contributing to their development.

The management of a business has no inherent rights other than those it continues to earn for itself year by year, through demonstrating its ability. It must select, train, and develop management people to cope with the political, social, and technical changes which face us today. This is the true criterion of management performance.

### LEARNING THROUGH PARTICIPATION

In our company we have been slowly learning the importance of having the next generation of our management people participate in the day-to-day challenges of the business, as a background for the future.

My office room includes the board table. I lunch there nearly every day, occasionally alone, but usually with a group of others selected on the basis of some company problem which needs handling, or some plan for the future. Unless too concentrated on the difficulty at hand to remember to do so, I add one, two, or three of our younger men to the luncheon list.

These lunches present a wonderful opportunity to broaden young men's understanding of management through the discussion of some serious problem. The discussions are completely informal and, at least to them, startlingly frank. Our own thinking has changed with the progress of time. We have come to realize that no effort can safely be spared from exposing the coming generation to the maximum of experience.

In the nineteen twenties some of our people thought our apprentice courses were not too bad — that, as companies went, we were doing quite well in the development of management material. The 1929–1934 period proved this an unfounded conceit. In three years we lost five of our six top people. There were no adequately trained successors for them, or for many of the others who dropped out. We promoted our own people, but it was tough going for them.

During the next period we seemed to be progressing. The war expansion, plus the scarcity of available younger men was again complete proof of overestimation of our success. There was a serious scarcity then, although we had successfully developed many of the men who entered the company as office boys, day laborers, molders, machinists. Many of these men were greatly helped by night school courses. For periods some alternated between plant work and school. But their number was not adequate.

Fortunately, the veterans who came back after the war not only were older, but also had matured beyond their years. Many of them developed more rapidly in the services than they would have had they remained in business. Many in a short period have advanced to positions of considerable management responsibility. The vacuum which pulled them forward filled quickly. Their records have built in us a still greater determination to do a better job of training in the future, and also to not allow the age of a man to interfere with his advancement.

It seems to have been a long, slow trip to where we are now, and there is a shock in the realization of how many more miles of needed progress lie ahead. Success depends on the kind of people in our ranks and on their enthusiasm for our objective—greater security for the people in the company and the owners for whom we all work. It will require still more concentration on our part to develop successfully men of the needed ability.

### DEVELOPING PEOPLE A RESPONSIBILITY OF EVERY EXECUTIVE

To succeed in the building of future managers, that cause must have high priority on the time and the planning of executives throughout the line of management. The development of an individual is a time-consuming job. It is necessary to know the man, to get to like him, and, liking him, to feel the duty to help build for him a success comparable with the potentials of his talents. The executive must travel the company circuit and see men function "on the job." If he is really interested, as someone has said, "He will even learn through the pores of his skin to understand men."

While it is true that there can be no ready-made system of education, there must be a broad program of development through guidance. The same is true of executive development. It must be a top-management concern, consistently and persistently pressed.

Any group with fair experience can sit around a table and lay out a sound executive development program. The problems are comparatively simple. But little is accomplished unless the heads of the company are bent on making the program succeed, determined day in and day out to keep pushing the cause. The president and all seniors must require a maximum interest and contribution from all who have to do with management. They must deal firmly with those in the management ranks who are laggard with respect to this important responsibility.

Those who are laggard in developing subordinates usually prove to have other weaknesses which have gone unnoticed. There have been many demotions from management places in the highest sales and operating positions because of men's failure to develop their people. These men were not big enough for their jobs. They did not have confidence enough in their people to let them carry the load of their jobs, functioning themselves as advisers.

### IMPORTANCE OF KNOWING JOB OUTLOOK

One of the most important factors in the development of people is the realization by the individual that if he does a good job it will be recognized. It is our policy to give our own people the benefit of advancement as openings occur. We believe that unless we have no one who can possibly qualify it is not fair to our people to hire an outsider merely because that outsider has held a high post in another company. To do so takes the most exciting element out of a man's work life.

The football player needs to know how many yards he has to go for a first down. So does the foreman need some idea of what is expected of him before he will qualify for the next opening for superintendent. All along the line the same applies. A man will not naturally exert himself to the limit until it is clear beyond any question that if he fills the bill he is reasonably sure of getting the promotion.

### BRAKE SHOE SETUP

It seems important in describing our plans to outline briefly the organization of Brake Shoe. We have 60 plants and, last December, employed 10,500 people. Plants average less than 150 employees, ranging from 30 to 550. Approximately 20 per cent are unskilled, 80 per cent skilled. There are 550 in supervision as superintendents, foremen, chief clerks. Sales people number nearly 250, research and engineering, 300.

There are ten different businesses, with ten managements, each with a president, one or more vice-presidents, a sales manager, and necessary department heads.

The company maintains a Service Division which includes Research, Purchasing, Accounting, Export, Construction and Maintenance, Safety and Hygiene, Labor Relations, Advertising, Secretary and Treasurer, Legal and other services. The Service Division, which I head, tries to relieve operating divisions of as many burdens as possible. This gives them maximum time to reduce costs, improve products, handle labor problems, and compete for a bigger portion of the available business.

### BRAKE SHOE MANAGEMENT APPRENTICES

Our thinking and experience in the development of management people may be clearer if I describe our program for management apprentices. Our greatest thrill has been to watch those who started as messenger boys or day laborers climb to important places. We have many such men — three started at thirteen.

Our apprentice-training approach illustrates the method we are using to develop people of all ages and in all areas of the organization. I am using the apprentice method as the simplest way to show our thinking and approach to the development of our people.

In any management-apprentice program four steps are important to success: (1) Selection; (2) Teaching; (3) Broadening through exposure; (4) Releasing talents.

The first step — selection of young men for training — is the most challenging one. In the first place it takes careful and effective planning to create a flow of top quality young men for employment interviews. It takes intelligence and patience in the interviews, for human beings are harder to judge than metal or wood. They cannot be X-rayed! But here again, you can't make a good product with poor material. This is just as true of turning out executives as of any other product.

It was in 1928 that our company first began selecting college seniors for future sales executives, operating managers, secretaries, treasurers, vice-presidents — and for my job. We wanted a management-trainee group — not just "more youngsters coming along." In making the selection, college courses and grades were item number one. But we also asked about his other activities. We inquired and guessed about the kind of person he was — yes, even the type of talents his ancestors possessed.

We were no longer only looking for a young man who could be trained for a certain place in operating, sales, or some other particular department. We were looking for men who seemed to be good gambles for the top echelon of management.

### SELECTING MANAGEMENT MATERIAL

In the process of searching for the right material, we had many discussions. Finally I tried to formulate a specification to use as an aid in judging these young men in terms of what management needs in people who are expected to climb in its ranks. This specification gave all of us concrete help in conducting our interviews. It was also useful to the young man, as he weighed what type of work best fitted him, and in which company his prospects would be best. It included such items as character, courage, common sense, ability to think and reason, imagination, initiative, resourcefulness, open-mindedness, and genuine interest in people.

In the specification we recommend guessing if he will *develop* into the kind of a man —

Who gets a real "kick" out of sticking his neck out — but not from a desire to show off
Who is keen to try a new way
Who enjoys proving that the boss is all wet
Who has the common sense to ask for outside help when he needs it, and the instinct to seek out the right person for that help
Who has unlimited confidence in the future, but is realistic about the terrible things that *can* happen
Who gets pleasure out of doing things for others
Who is challenged by tough problems
Who will be a useful citizen
Who realizes that all men want and need friendships
Who is not afraid of being afraid.

There are many other points in the specification.

We believe and practice that several of us are better than any one of us when it comes to judging a young man — as to the talents and wisdom he will develop, where he will best fit, how he can best develop his full capabilities. So it is our practice to pass around the young man who is being considered, and who is considering us, letting him talk with officers and executives in various departments and with some of our younger men. If, ultimately, he comes to work for us, the type of work he is to do is left to him and to the man who will be his boss.

Keen competition has developed in our company in this selective process. Each of us boasts of his correct guesses and gets a fair amount of "ribbing" for his mistakes. We all enjoy "taking a look" at the prospective apprentice. Each of us tries hard to help him make a correct decision. In passing, I would like to observe that, in our experience, normally the younger members of the organization are the best guessers.

If the young man feels inclined to join us, and we like him, our suggestion often is that he take a look at some of our plants and talk with the superintendents. At each plant that he visits, his guide is an apprentice or a youngster recently graduated from the course. He is also given opportunities to talk with other apprentices and supervisors. Such steps not only increase the chances of a correct decision, but also make a favorable impression on him. We have had cases where three, four, or even five of our ten divisions were competing for a young man. And we tell him when this occurs.

PROVIDING GOOD TEACHERS

Step number two in a sound executive development program is providing the youngsters who join our ranks with good teachers. It is as important for us to be effective teachers as it is for the members of any college faculty.

We awoke much too slowly to the fact that the development of individuals was frequently retarded and often defeated by supervisory people who did not understand teaching, or were not really interested in helping the people under them to make personal progress. As a by-product we came to realize that generally a poor teacher of apprentices is a poor developer of molders, machinists, and certainly of foremen. And the same is true of the developing of material in the office.

Concentration on laying the groundwork for developing management people highlighted some important misconceptions. For example, in the old days the best salesman usually moved up to sales manager. Our idea today is that the sales manager's number one job is developing salesmen, not personal selling. The "born salesman" type normally ignores his teaching job. He feels the customer needs him — personally. The sales manager who concentrates on developing his men is interested in helping them to plan their selling. He takes over only when invited by a salesman to do so. He devotes his time to teaching, realizing its long-range importance.

In all departments we found it necessary first to crystallize company feeling as to the importance of teaching; second, to help the teachers to a better understanding of teaching.

It took us a long time to realize that men who contribute to the building of an individual merit recognition of that fact in their salary. Currently we have many people in operating and sales-management positions whose pay checks reflect their success in augmenting individual competence. I fear most of these increases are too small to be just. During the recent period of salary raises for all, some men's salaries have lagged because they couldn't or wouldn't teach. Here our courage in penalizing has not rated medals.

In reverse, we have become convinced that men not deeply interested in increasing the competence of others also lack the degree of "cause-mindedness" which is essential to maximum success. People who do not believe that furthering the general cause adds most to their individual progress are definitely not right people for any organization with forward-looking objectives.

Apprentice-training programs probably exist in most American companies of any size. Generally they are good plans, carefully developed through trial and error within the company, coupled with a study of the experiences of other companies. Actually, as we all know, an excellent training plan of itself accomplishes nothing. The impact on the beginner from the people who work over him is much more important than the plan. It is obvious, of course, that success in developing any individual requires a basic feeling of friendship toward him. To teach well requires the heart as well as the head.

With ten separate businesses our development plan is run by ten management groups. The Research Department makes it eleven. Each has its own beginners' course.

On an average, each currently has five apprentices. Obviously, the training methods are based on small groups, comparable to a tutoring school rather than to college classes. This gives great elasticity and makes adaptation to the individual easy. But, on the negative side, eleven management groups must be made to function effectively in training the new generation. There are premiums for successes and penalties for failures.

Plant training for sales averages one year and for plant operating positions two years. In each department the apprentice is a worker, not an observer. He is encouraged to make suggestions as to his own training. He suggests longer or shorter periods in departments according to his feeling of the need. His group has as advisor an ex-apprentice, with whom the members meet monthly for discussion of their work. Every six weeks the advisor arranges a half-day meeting with a division executive for further discussion of problems and progress. At these meetings each is encouraged to ask questions.

Toward the end of the preparation of salesmen the apprentices are taken on field trips with salesmen and service calls with engineers. Depending on the work for which they are being trained, they spend a period in the engineering and research department of the company. They have a period in the sales office observing company policy at work, seeing sales problems and their handling, getting a picture of how customer relations function.

Teaching cannot be sporadic. It must be carried on consistently. It must continue until the man reaches the end of his company career. Only by sustained effort can we develop the full effectiveness of which each man is capable.

There is one teaching method we use which may be of interest. It was started for the education of the officer group. From time to time eight or ten of the younger men who have completed their apprenticeship courses and have had a year or two in sales, operating, or purchasing, are invited to the New York office for a series of three or four meetings. At their first meeting a company officer explains briefly that as a result of their group discussions the company hopes many criticisms and suggestions based on their individual experiences can be relayed anonymously to management, covering such topics as:

1. Where and in what ways the handling of apprentices as individuals is poor
2. How the apprenticeship course can be improved
3. Where and how the general philosophies and policies as set forth in company talks are not being carried out by plant managers, foremen, sales managers, etc.

They are told quite sincerely that no holds are barred. The officer leaves and the group then meets by itself. After a series of follow-up meetings the group submits minutes of its discussions to the management. The results to date have been most helpful. We have learned of many faults, some of which we were not conscious of.

As an important by-product of these meetings, the participants are given an opportunity:

1. For self-analysis — how they are doing in relation to the others. This is measured by what they know of Brake Shoe and its policies, by their sense of loyalty, by their attitude toward their bosses, and by many other factors
2. To reappraise their bosses and others working with them

in the light of the other participants' appraisals of their bosses

3. To be better prepared for an executive position when that day comes.

BROADENING THE EXPERIENCE

The third step in executive development is widening the range of the man's experience. This means giving him an opportunity to observe how men in many departments handle their problems. That is why we aim to have men spend time in the general offices visiting different departments, getting a chance to understand the function of each. We are trying to build in our people a comprehensive background for their field work, so that they will be more effective in giving the customer a picture of our company; and so that with better understanding they will develop more rapidly into potential management material.

We regard apprentice courses as only Step Number One in the education of future managers, just as obtaining a law school education is the first step in preparing men for the practice of law. In both, effectiveness depends on continuous effort throughout their work life to learn more and to keep current with the endlessly changing conditions which must be met. In business this means maximum exposure of the individual to every type of company problem.

The best experience is gained through the fullest possible association of promising men with their seniors of every rank. Out in the plant apprentices and junior executives can observe foremen handling human relations, and learn the meaning of kindness, friendship, and integrity. In the office they can sit in on discussions of important policy matters. A continuous exposure to all phases of the business is essential to developing men for the highest echelons.

With this in mind we try to remember to ask one or two of the younger men from different departments to sit in on:

A labor negotiation at the plant
A battle over advertising copy
A product pricing argument
A discussion with lawyers
A financing negotiation
Pension system planning
A discussion of what subjects should be covered in the annual report to stockholders.

Our plan is to give them maximum exposure to developing plans and making decisions. This not only helps them prepare for the future but improves their day-to-day carry on. It helps develop their talents and increase their wisdom. Seeing us in the midst of making mistakes helps build their self-confidence.

We have found that the board room table is one of our best tools of exposure. Over "cold-cuts," a bowl of mixed green salad, and a piece of French pastry or pie, you can expose men to the problems of many different phases of the business. And during this exposure you can size a man up and learn more about how he can be helped. You can tell much about the young by the way they react to what is said.

There are many methods of exposure. In our company—with ten divisions, ten separate managements, each running a business — there is often the opportunity to transfer a man from one department to another. For example, a successful purchasing officer may be shifted to a general management place. Or a man who has moved up in accounting may be transferred to sales management. Giving men of talent new exposures broadens their experience and helps them qualify for higher places. In the past three years, for example, twenty-five of our young men have been transferred from Research to various operating departments.

Broadening is also achieved by adding a new responsibility to a man's department — such as transferring supervision of the Safety and Hygiene Department to the Treasurer. These added responsibilities gave him an excellent schooling in the relations of people as they work together in plants and offices.

It is surprising how many improvements in management come out of the things that go wrong. For many years we had pushed the education of our operating supervisors, encouraging their exposure to all phases of company problems. But more and more I realized that our efforts to this end weren't meeting with success. Accordingly, at a meeting of division heads two years ago, we decided on a series of meetings which we are now conducting each month for foremen, chief clerks, and superintendents from our plants all over the country. These four-day meetings of small groups are designed to expose these management people to the whys and wherefores of our policies and practices. They are held to inform — not to pep up — our people. As far as possible there is only one man from each plant at a meeting.

At these meetings different executives tell how the work of their department relates to the business as a whole. The men are encouraged to ask questions, and no sensible question goes unanswered. The utmost frankness prevails. Some questions create a feeling of inadequacy — are literally dumbfounding.

For example: "Mr. Given, you spoke of building greater security for company people as the first objective. Then why was Harry Schultz fired after 18 years of service, with four promotions during that time?" The facts must prove that for the good of the company Harry Schultz could not be kept.

That reminds me of a vital point. Lately at these and other meetings I have been emphasizing the unfairness of not frankly criticizing the man under you, thus giving him fundamental help in improving his performance. To me this is one of business management's greatest failures. I believe it exists to too great an extent in all companies.

At these meetings the men are gaining greater understanding and competence. They receive a broader picture of company problems and policies. By associating with each other their development is accelerated. They are being qualified for higher positions. On the other hand, the questions they raise educate the company's executives and make them better teachers.

Two or three times a year there is a meeting of division presidents. Each brings one of his head people and often a junior. The meetings last two days. Discussions cover every phase of current problems, future prospects, and, yes, hopes. There is little talk about yesterday. Many decisions are made. Many plans are made more concrete. The juniors get a complete picture of the wide gamut of problems which need attention. They also get an intimate view of the qualifications of each of us as an advisor on the different problems he will meet.

#### RELEASING TALENTS

Exposure to different phases of a business is all important in developing executives, but it accomplishes little if we do not release the individual's talents. We must see that bosses all down the line develop men's initiative and give them authority to decide and act. This is the fourth essential to the successful development of effective management people. We must be willing to gamble, and not let men's youth make us cautious.

Capable men usually have many abilities. In doing everything in our power to bring in winners, we must gamble on their broader abilities as opportunities for advancement occur. We must give our best to coaching and encouraging them, spending what time is necessary. In most cases men who show the capacity to improve one department have the same impact on another. There are exceptions, but we must not let mistakes make cowards of us. For when the man does succeed, each new advance adds greatly to his competence to move still higher. We have learned not to limit the man's experience to his special field.

Two of our divisions are headed by an ex-general purchasing agent. Four in the Purchasing Department were in operating jobs. The Treasurer became, as an extra responsibility, head of the Safety and Hygiene Department. The former head of Safety is sales assistant to the president. Superintendents have been moved from manganese foundries to heat-resistant material plants. Superintendents have become salesmen. Conversely, a salesman has become an operating head.

We believe that if a man has learned to handle one function successfully there is definite indication that he can grapple successfully with a different one, perhaps with several.

Being born with many talents is not fundamental to success. The talents a man adds are more important. The work of management is to help the individual to discover and develop his talents. We can help the man with his planning, but we should always leave him the maximum elasticity in execution.

Business life is limited for men who avoid responsibility. One of the great needs of business is for men who reach out for more. We can help such men by being at their side whenever possible. Their part is self-education; our part is guidance and the broadening of their experience through ours. We can augment their courage with ours; it takes courage on our part to give them latitude to fail.

### IMPORTANCE OF AN EARLY START

In the development of managers, it is important that a man's first position of responsibility come early in his business life. The more years of experience he has had in making decisions, the greater will be his wisdom and usually the higher his courage when he reaches the top ranks. By then he has become accustomed to making mistakes. And out of that experience he is more willing to try new ways and to give those around him the freedom to suggest and decide — and to make mistakes.

High courage and wisdom are qualities that come to the normal man only through years of responsibility. Emerson said, "Courage consists of equality to the problem before us." Freedom to make mistakes builds courage by developing a feeling of equality. The cautious in life too often prove to be those who gambled by being too cautious.

To help in the development of an individual's talents, to assist in his acquisition of wisdom and courage, much time must be devoted to the exchange of ideas and experiences between the man and his teachers. To accomplish most, there must be that mutual confidence which releases frankness.

As teachers we must, above all, endeavor to develop wisdom in those we train for management's ranks. Wisdom will come to a man from analyzing his failures and successes. But to an even greater degree it can come from an understanding of the successes and failures of others. We can help our people build wisdom through our own experiences, provided we are honest about our mistakes. Coleridge wrote, "Wisdom is common sense to an uncommon degree." We must add to their talents the base for a greater degree of common sense.

Able people in a business have the incentive to give their best to the cause only if promotions are generally from within the ranks. Time and again all of us have seen the effect on company personnel where the opposite occurs frequently. If a company sincerely wishes to succeed in developing executives it will promote from within to the maximum extent possible. Even when men seem not to be fully qualified, the company must gamble on them. For only by going all out on this policy can the company successfully develop the individual's full competence. This calls for the highest degree of management faith. But success in developing people also brings to management its greatest thrill.

## LEADERSHIP IN AN EVOLVING ORGANIZATION

BY

*Joseph B. Hall*

PRESIDENT

THE KROGER COMPANY

CINCINNATI, OHIO

One of the responsibilities of every executive who heads a business is to keep the business in tune with the times: equipped to meet the wants of customers, the challenge of competitors, and the impact of other external forces.

In discharging this responsibility, the chief executive must make certain that the business is properly organized and that the positions provided by the plan of organization are staffed with properly qualified individuals. During a period when the plan of organization must be changed rapidly to meet new conditions, it may not always be possible to find just the right people in the business to staff the new positions.

Under these conditions, there must be a balance struck. The plan of organization must be modified to fit the executive personnel available. The executives available must be assigned skillfully so as to utilize their talents to the full. Training and retraining can be used to help in striking the most effective balance and in overcoming the shortcomings of personnel.

Using his own company as an illustration, Mr. Hall deals concretely with these problems in this section. He describes the program Kroger has followed in coping with changing internal and external conditions through changes in organization and reassignment and retraining of executive personnel. The principles he outlines and the methods he describes are applicable to every business.

Mr. Hall graduated from the University of Chicago in 1921. After ten years of experience in real estate and banking, he joined the Kroger Company in 1931 as manager of the real estate department. Four years later, he transferred to the retail division and, after a period of training in the stores, became manager of one of the large branches.

From that position, he advanced to division manager and in 1941 was named vice-president in charge of manufacturing and elected a director. He became treasurer in 1943, executive vice-president in 1944, and president in 1946.

Mr. Hall is a member of the board of directors of the Cincinnati branch of the Federal Reserve Bank of Cleveland, president of the Citizen Development Committee of Cincinnati, vice-president of the Ohio State Council of Retail Merchants, and a member of the Executive Board of the National Association of Food Chains.

Under Mr. Hall's leadership, The Kroger Company, one of the country's largest food chains, has inaugurated a number of forward-looking policies in chain-store management.

When the New York City subway system was new, O. Henry, the short-story writer, wisecracked: "Rapid transit gloria mundi." But whether we say "rapid transit" or "sic transit," we will all admit that the glories of the world *are* fleeting and that we live in a changing universe in which evolution is a basic law.

### BUSINESSES MUST ADAPT TO CHANGE

The law of constant change applies as fully to the life of a business as to the life of a man. The business which cannot adapt itself to an altered environment is a business whose prosperity will vanish as conditions change.

Early in the present century, for example, most of our wagon-building companies were sadly damaged by the arrival of the automobile. But one such company — Studebaker — accepted evolution by manufacturing automobiles; and it made a great deal more money out of horseless carriages than it had ever made on vehicles with four-legged propulsion.

It follows, then, that one of the fundamental tests of business leadership is the ability of that leadership to adapt the business to changing conditions. So I am going to deal first with some of the changes that have taken place in the Kroger business, and some of the ways in which these changes have been met by evolution in the Kroger organization. I will deal also with balancing personalities within an organization, since theoretically correct organization charts cannot always be put into effect.

And finally, I should like to leave you with some idea of the Kroger organization's most distinguishing feature —leadership through understanding. To an unusual extent our twenty-six retail branches are self-governing, autonomous units. And our general office operates by suggestion rather than by command.

CHANGE IN THE KROGER SETUP

In 1929 the Kroger Company operated more than 5600 stores. In 1949 we are operating nearer 2300. At first sight we might seem to be disappearing rather than evolving. But let me hasten to add that whereas in 1929 our average store did a business of about $1000 a *week*, our average store now does a business of over $1000 a *day*. From a 1929 volume of $286,000,000 we have progressed to a 1948 volume of $825,000,000. And our 1948 net was $9,300,000 against $5,900,000 in 1929.

The trend toward fewer but very much larger units has been a very successful trend. It has been accentuated by the development of the self-service store, which has enabled a small number of store people to serve a large number of customers, and by the manner in which the automobile has expanded the trading area of each Kroger unit.

The large store unit—the so-called supermarket—compelled us to make a basic change in store organization and to create a position which we had never had before: the Kroger Store Manager. Until four years ago there was no such position as a Kroger Store Manager. Instead, we had in each store a grocery manager and a meat manager. The grocery manager looked after everything but the meat department. But the meat manager was supreme in his own field. And neither manager was in any sense the boss of the other or the boss of the store. This separation of groceries and meats was maintained not only in the stores; it ran straight up through the organization — grocery supervisors and meat supervisors, branch grocery operators and branch meat operators.

The dual arrangement no doubt seems peculiar to you; indeed it *now* seems peculiar to us. Certainly it had few, if any, redeeming traits. A store is a unit; it is not a Siamese twin. Dual management made it difficult to allocate expenses and almost impossible to allocate responsibility. If a store was losing money, the grocery manager blamed the meat manager, and vice versa; if it was making money, each manager thought that the credit belonged largely, if not entirely, to him. Nevertheless, the double-management setup was once universal in chain stores and still prevails in some chain organizations.

Like many other anomalies, the presence of a grocery manager and a meat manager, and the absence of a store manager, was chiefly an accident of history. When the late B. H. Kroger opened the first — and, of course, the only — Kroger store in 1882, he sold nothing but dry groceries. Indeed, food chain stores began chiefly as tea and coffee specialty shops. Mr. Kroger originally did business under the name of The Great Western Tea Company — and even such staples as flour and potatoes were not added for some time.

And although Kroger was one of the first grocery chains

— perhaps the *first* — to go into the meat business, meats were not included until 1901 — thirty years after the foundation of the company. They arrived not because Mr. Kroger decided, as a matter of policy, that meats would be a valuable addition to Kroger merchandise, but because Mr. Kroger had the opportunity to buy a group of meat stores. Thus meat arrived as a stranger within the gates and remained so until very recent times. Indeed, about 500 of our 2300 stores are even now operating without a meat department, although these are nearly all older and smaller stores which represent yesterday rather than today.

With the exception of these comparatively few stores, however, we now operate with store managers, and operate much more efficiently than under the department-manager setup. The store manager thinks in terms of a store, not of a department. He may be held responsible if the store makes a poor showing, but he will receive the credit if the store is a success. In smaller towns, he may well be one of the community's leading citizens and businessmen. In large cities, he may have from 20 to 50 men and women working under him; his cash register may ring up sales of $20,000 a week or more.

The store manager is in direct line for promotion — perhaps to district manager (a man who supervises the operation of several stores); perhaps to a merchandising job in the branch office. His pay may range from $60 to $125 a week and he is considered a member of management, not a part of the general working force. Single-man control is so superior to the department-manager setup that now we wonder why the old system hung on for so many years.

BRINGING ABOUT THE CHANGE

Yet the one-store, one-manager policy was not established by any sudden order from on high. In fact, the change first was made in the supervision of stores. This was a process of evolution. Twenty years ago meat supervisors were responsible for a group of meat departments and grocery supervisors for grocery departments, with little coördination at the store level. Then the position of district manager was established. The district manager, with the help of a meat assistant and a grocery assistant, had supervision over a group of stores. But we still had the Siamese twins — the two uncoördinated departments in the stores themselves, and the two district assistants who passed the buck from one to the other.

Reason finally prevailed. Districts were made smaller and one man became responsible for all departments in the group of stores under his supervision. Top management made the suggestion. One branch adopted the idea and put it into successful effect. Based on this success, other branches followed. Through discussions with branch managers and the four division managers, who are each responsible for a group of branches, the single line district manager plan was adopted by all branches. The program evolved over a period of months. It was effected through leadership — not forced by edict.

This set the pattern for the stores and over-all store management was gradually established. Here again the program was initiated in one branch, then extended to the other branches in one division, and finally throughout the company. Again the idea was "sold." No order was given.

The branch manager established the program in his branch only when he was convinced of its soundness.

DEVELOPMENT THROUGH TRAINING

The task of "selling" was somewhat slow. The training job was even slower. Meat men were trained in the grocery business and grocery men in the meat business. The training courses were developed by bringing together men from the branches who applied the principles of wartime "Job Instruction Training"—breaking down the jobs into their parts and developing a training program to stress the key points.

With the advent of self-service it was necessary to add checker training, produce training, and dairy department training in order to round out the program. No textbooks are used in Kroger. Training in its various phases follows prepared outlines and these outlines are kept up to date by constant revision.

Basic training starts in the store. This consists of handling produce, meats, groceries, and cashier operations. Instruction is first given in classrooms where store conditions are approximated. Classroom work is followed by actual store experience with proper follow-up by the trainer. Job assignment follows.

Employees are constantly studied and rated for further training and advancement. Training for store department heads and managers includes a visit to branch headquarters for interview by various branch executives. These visits not only furnish the trainee with advice and counsel, but also enable branch executives to judge his ability and the progress he is making. The district managers are selected from the store managers, although special college trainee groups have been developed to supplement the store-manager material. Junior key men, sales promotion and buying assistants frequently develop from the stores. Up to this point, most of the advancement is in terms of the individual branch.

Now opportunity is broadened. Groups of men are brought into the general office for three-day or five-day broadening and training courses. These men are selected by the branch managers, with the advice of the division managers, from the district men and the branch key personnel. These sessions enable the men under observation to demonstrate their thinking ability, their merchandising sense, and ability to present ideas to others. At the same time, executives in general office become acquainted with these promotional prospects. The experienced trainers and personnel men can observe these candidates for advancement closely and form opinions concerning their capabilities.

From these groups men are selected for "on the job" training. Specific responsibility is given to them. Their training occurs in two or three branches other than their "home" branch, which gives them the benefit of broader experience. Their activities in these branches and in general office, plus the opinion of the executives in their "home" branch, together form the basis for their subsequent advancement.

The trainee-group is reviewed constantly by the divisional men and the general manager of operations in consultation with the director of personnel. The procedure exposes the trainees to a large group of men so that their advancement opportunities are company-wide.

Similar procedures are followed for men in the specialized fields of accounting, real estate, personnel, warehousing, and manufacturing. In these specialized groups, we look continuously for men who can be transferred to other phases of the business so that opportunity is not restricted to their specialized field. Much emphasis is placed on training in several fields to broaden the individual and develop him for over-all management.

The training process continues at all times and at all levels. The training program is kept practical by bringing men from operations into the position of trainer. The instruction of others has proven to be an excellent method of broadening the instructors, and men with experience as trainers are placed back in operations, usually in positions of greater responsibility. The experiences of actual operation are thus brought constantly into training and the benefits of training taken back into operations. Training thus does not become stereotyped.

Effort is made constantly to train men in various phases of our business. Men from the retail branches are placed with our nation-wide produce-buying organization to bring the sales viewpoint to the field of buying. Similarly, branch men are brought into the general office so as to bring the problems of the field closer to the central direction of activities. Men are transferred from branch to branch, from branch field operation to branch office operation, and from grocery to meat to produce merchandising jobs. This varied responsibility trains the executive to meet changing conditions which have occurred and will continue to occur in our business.

### ADAPTING THE PLAN TO THE PEOPLE

A comparison of the Kroger organization chart for 1931 with that for 1949 would show the extent to which our present plan has been an evolutionary development. I doubt if the best firm of management consultants — and we had one of the best — could have established a plan of organization in 1931 which would have been effective today. The change in our business has been too great.

Even at a given moment, an ideal plan of organization frequently cannot be put into effect due to inability to secure the necessary executives immediately, or to the undesirability of making too many or too rapid personnel changes. After proper study, or in consultation with management consultants, top management may arrive at the ideal organization plan. The specifications for the various positions may be written and the relationships established between them. It is well that this be done. Then comes the problem of implementing the plan. Consideration must be given to men available within the company as well as those who may be brought in from the outside to strengthen the personnel — and it is at times necessary to bring in outsiders, even though every effort is made to develop executives from within.

It would be fortuitous if every position were filled with the ideal man. To my knowledge, this has never happened at Kroger. I doubt if it has occurred ever in any large organization. Individuals have both strengths and weaknesses. Their strengths should be utilized. Their weaknesses should be balanced by the abilities of other men who are teamed up with them. Balancing of abilities is all-important in any organization. An organization too strong in selling may sell itself into bankruptcy. An organization too control-minded may gradually dry up.

### AN ILLUSTRATION OF BALANCING

Another basic change in Kroger operations came with the shift in emphasis from buying to selling. Until the past few years, we operated on a functional basis with one man responsible for buying and another man responsible for selling. Sometimes there was friction between these men. If, for instance, merchandise failed to sell, the sales promotion man claimed that the merchandise was inferior; whereupon the buyer would intimate that the sales promotion man had missed his true vocation and should be farming or cleaning the streets. The situation was somewhat like that between the meat managers and the grocery managers; in both cases it was difficult to hold men responsible when each man handled only a part of the complete job.

So, instead of a buyer and a seller, we made one man both buyer and seller and called him a merchandiser. He became responsible for the sale of everything he bought. The new setup was a great improvement because the merchandiser, as much concerned with sales as with purchases, followed through on his merchandise until it reached the customers' kitchens.

In implementing this plan, we were confronted with utilization of capable men within the organization. Some men were enthusiastic sales promotion men able to sell ideas and products. Others were capable buyers with detailed knowledge of markets and market trends. Few men were capable in both fields. We selected the strongest men. Where their strengths lay in the promotional field, we balanced them with a good analytical buying assistant. Where their strengths lay in market and product knowledge, we supplemented them with a sales promotion assistant. It is important at all times to maintain a proper balance. And special care must be taken to see that balance is maintained when changes are made due to advancement or separation of individuals.

This balancing of abilities is important not only in the merchandising field but throughout an organization. It becomes even more important at the top management level. Failure to recognize its importance and provide for proper balance frequently produces unnecessary friction and unsatisfactory results.

### EXERCISING LEADERSHIP THROUGH GAINING UNDERSTANDING

We, in Kroger, try to manage through developing understanding as a result of discussions rather than through giving a series of orders. At Kroger we recognize two kinds of responsibility — vertical responsibility and horizontal responsibility. Vertical responsibility is the type of responsibility that is found in all sizable organizations. In our company it centers in the field men and flows from the general manager of operations, to the division manager, the branch manager, the district manager, and the store manager. This is the line along which instructions flow and — we trust — are followed through.

Horizontal responsibility centers in the merchandising

groups and staff departments in general office. Their responsibility is more than advisory. We look to the merchandising departments for sales, gross profit, and inventory control. We look to the personnel department for developing sufficient candidates for positions in the company; to the real estate department for establishment of proper store programs. This functional responsibility is exercised through leadership — through instructions and suggestions, by projecting plans and ideas, by building confidence. Ideas are "sold" — orders are not given. There is no line authority for this group.

Friction develops at times through our recognition of both vertical and horizontal responsibilities; but this friction is a result of initiative on the part of the various departments rather than resentment because of too many orders. It can nearly always be resolved by top executive vigilance and action. Every effort is made to develop maximum initiative through attaining an understanding of policies and programs and then allowing the executives to exercise their judgment rather than restricting them to carrying out orders.

Development of understanding was the main activity of the British War Cabinet. The operation of the Cabinet was outlined in mimeographed material sent to Mr. Forrestal, former Secretary of Defense. He allowed me to borrow it two years ago when I was studying organizational problems. Mr. Forrestal was attempting to pattern the United States military defense along the lines of the effective British organization. The War Cabinet, composed of top men in armed services, industry, and governmental positions, met frequently to discuss problems until an understanding was reached as to the course of action to be taken. The Cabinet, as such, issued no orders. Each individual in his field of activity would carry out this understanding to the best of his ability, with the least restriction on his efforts.

To a large extent, Kroger also functions in this manner Through discussions we arrive at certain policies or programs. By means of meetings we develop an understanding of this program. We then expect the men in the various fields of responsibility to carry out the program. Specific orders frequently limit a man's scope to carrying out only what is called for in the order. When a man understands a general program and is given a reasonably free hand in carrying it out, he may make a much broader contribution to the program's success. This applies not only in the relationship of the staff departments to the field — horizontal responsibility — but in the line responsibilities running from the general office to branch, to districts, and to stores. Many meetings are held to develop an understanding of the problems involved and the solutions suggested.

Let us say that a policy or a program originates with the general office merchandisers. This policy or program is not, however, established until it has been thoroughly discussed with division and branch merchandisers, and with division and branch managers. We expect that the man who does not approve the suggested policy or program will express his objections in a clear and audible voice, and we are very rarely disappointed in this expectation. It is true that after a proposal has been thoroughly gone into, and the majority are clearly in favor of it, we then do expect everybody to put his shoulder to the wheel. But many an idea that seemed good to its originator when he thought it up, has been torn to pieces at divisional and branch meetings.

The process of developing the facts, discussing the problem, and selling it to the organization requires more time, patience and effort than the process of issuing orders. On the other hand, it encourages initiative, it diminishes the chances of error, and it guarantees that programs are being carried out by men who are sold on them.

The manner in which we arrived at our general sales and operational program for 1949 is a good example of decisions developed through consultation. We were confronted with the problem of how to meet increased 1949 expenses in the face of a probably diminishing 1949 sales volume. We figured expenses as closely as possible — no calculations involving the future can ever be exact. We made sales estimates, based on the best figures available. We then projected profit figures, and found them unsatisfactory.

The situation was first discussed with the officers of the company. Then came a joint meeting with merchandisers and divisional men. Steps to overcome the poor results indicated were discussed and some tentative conclusions were reached. Then we assembled the 26 branch managers, acquainted them with the problem confronting us, and invited suggestions for improving the indicated results. In the course of an all-day meeting, a program was developed which we believe will overcome increasing expenses and make 1949 a satisfactory year.

This program still was tentative. It was taken by the

branch managers to their branches for discussion with their executive groups and served as the basis for each branch to develop its program for 1949. And this 1949 program is a program largely developed by the branches — by the field men who will be charged with putting it into effect. It is a program developed through discussion and understanding — not imposed upon the branches by orders from on high.

The Kroger organization is not perfect and I am sure that it never will be. But I am equally sure it will be led by a group of executives who are alive to changing conditions and who will constantly study policies and procedures to see where changes should be made. Executives will be chosen for the abilities most vital to their jobs; and their work will be balanced by associating them with men who possess supplementary and complementary capacities.

Understanding of our policies and programs will be developed through meetings and discussion. Every encouragement will be given to initiative, self-reliance, and independent thought. Thus we hope to develop a dynamic, fluid, adaptable leadership to cope with a present that is vitally different from the past and a future that will be, no doubt, quite as different from the present.

# SELF-DEVELOPMENT FOR BUSINESS LEADERSHIP

BY

*George S. Dively*

PRESIDENT

HARRIS-SEYBOLD COMPANY

CLEVELAND, OHIO

No executive gets an opportunity to discharge the responsibilities of business leadership unless he attains a leadership position. That means that he must attain leadership recognition in his own enterprise or so conduct himself in one enterprise that his leadership will be sought by another.

In the final analysis, therefore, none of the responsibilities, opportunities, or challenges to business leaders which were dealt with in the previous sections come into play until the individual has attained that position in some enterprise. Whether an individual does attain a position of business leadership depends upon his own basic qualifications and how he handles himself in the group with which he is associated. It is of great importance to the nation, and of course to the individual himself, that an increasing number of business executives develop leadership qualities. The development of these qualities can be learned. Certainly, the individual who possesses the basic qualifications of leadership can learn to exploit them more fully and so speed up the process of attaining business leadership.

In this section, Mr. Dively comes to grips with the attainment of leadership from the standpoint of the individual. He outlines the qualifications the business leader must develop; suggests and illustrates how the developmental process should be carried on; and even deals with tactical problems in the development of executive leadership.

Although somewhat reluctant to do so, Mr. Dively was persuaded to deal with the individual development of leadership in this fashion, basing his contribution on experience as well as analysis.

Mr. Dively is a graduate of the Engineering School of the University of Pittsburgh and of the Harvard Graduate School of Business Administration, class of 1929. He worked up to become assistant general works manager of North American Refractories Company and then was a partner in an investment banking firm, a sales executive with the Carrier Corporation, and an industrial engineer with Republic Steel Corporation, before joining his present company as assistant to the treasurer about twelve years ago. Then he was successively assistant treasurer, secretary-treasurer, vice-president and general manager; he has been president and general manager since 1947.

Among various association activities, Mr. Dively is a director of the American Management Association and was previously vice-president in charge of the production division of that Association. He is president of the Cleveland Branch of the National Metal Trades Association and a past president of the Cleveland Control of the Controllers Institute.

It is generally recognized that, in terms of the individual, the qualities of business leadership are highly complex. In this area of human understanding there has been all too little research, and real knowledge is quite limited. Therefore, many of my deductions must be based on personal observation and experience. And I present them with a feeling of humility.

In developing himself as a business leader, it seems to me that a man should give particular consideration to these four general areas:

1. Personality and character traits
2. Working with people
3. Making decisions
4. Developing and selling ideas.

### PERSONALITY AND CHARACTER TRAITS

Although more and more material on personality and character traits is becoming available, I consider purposeful energy, progressiveness, intensity, and health as being particularly necessary to the business leader.

Purposeful energy is commonly reflected in enthusiasm, initiative, and optimism; these traits are so much a natural part of leadership that it is quite unusual to find them lacking.

Progressiveness is often reflected in the ease of generating and accepting new ideas. However, the leader learns to moderate progressiveness by conservatism under some conditions, and by patience and humility under others. Incidentally, during an executive's early experience it is usually beneficial for him to cultivate patience and humbleness as counterbalances to natural youthful tendencies toward immature progressiveness.

Intensity and drive are characteristics of the outstanding executive which make him and his job almost one. A real leader reflects his job, and the job reflects his personality. The inseparable nature of the two probably results from the depth and consistency of attention to his job.

Health is a factor of growing importance. The requirements of business leadership are becoming more exacting and complex, and the tempo continues to rise. The increasing frequency of hypertension, heart ailments, and stomach ulcers among business executives, particularly those of middle age, should be viewed with alarm. Counterdevelopments appear essential. More real relaxation, better planned vacations, and greater hobby interests are certainly desirable. Thought might also be given to building greater inner-contentment and a better philosophy of living.

In considering such traits as fairness and mental honesty, it is what the other fellow thinks that counts. Personal standards are developed in time. A leader needs a standard that people look up to. Other traits such as appearance, manner, habits, and social status do not make a business leader; but noticeable weaknesses in any of these traits can deter and sometimes nullify otherwise good executive development.

In general there is, of course, some question as to how much we can change our established personality and character traits. However, we should try to recognize accurately those traits which most commonly and predominately appear in business leadership. We can learn to use those we have to advantage — to accentuate the positive. And we can try to offset weaknesses by cultivating associates and bringing into our respective organizations subordinates with supplementary traits.

### WORKING WITH PEOPLE

In any study of self-development for business leadership, it would be hard to overemphasize the importance of working with people, that is, the ability to get things done through people. This aspect of leadership can be approached from three principal angles: working with your superior, working with your associates, and working with your subordinates.

1. *Working with your superior:* Loyalty is one item in working with your superior that requires careful consideration and a nice balance. It should be given freely when the superior deserves and earns it. In fact, he should be given the benefit of all reasonable doubt. Loyalty, however, should not be for sale through favors. Nor should a superior expect loyalty from a subordinate which involves basic conflict with loyalty to the company. The subordinate's relationship with his superior was well expressed by Diogenes when he said: "We should live with our superior as with fire: not too near lest we burn; not too far off, lest we freeze."

Insubordination on the other hand cannot be tolerated

if the leader's respect and control are to be maintained. A subordinate should charge himself with full responsibility for not getting into a position of insubordination, except, of course, in instances where generally accepted basic principles are clearly infringed.

Dependability and follow-through probably constitute two of the strongest measures of effectiveness in working with your superior. Initiative and doing more than expected perhaps make the best sales approach for a subordinate in building himself up in the eyes of his superior. It is always constructive to help the superior by supplementing his weaknesses, particularly when this can be handled with a reasonable degree of finesse and understanding.

2. *Working with your associates:* Make yourself easy to get acquainted with and to work with — loosen up — be adaptable. Be alert to your associates' attitudes — develop sensitivity. Learn how they react and what motivates them — develop objectivity.

Learn to identify and understand areas of more or less natural conflict between you and your associates. Such an area may exist between men with a full background of formal education and not much practical experience and those with many years of good, practical experience but with little, if any, formal education. A combination of good experience and good education has proved to be the best basis for proper solutions to most business problems. Therefore, learn to recognize the contributions of associates who have good, practical experience but little formal education. You need the benefit of their experience. They need the benefit of your education. Each should learn to use the contributions of the other. This is a mark of business leadership.

Show interest in your associates; seek advice from them; and go out of your way to help them. The modern business organization, with its highly developed staff and committee supplements to the line organization, requires much cross reference. It helps a lot to be on effective working terms with your associates. Considerable cultivation will pay off.

3. *Working with your subordinates:* In working with subordinates, it is generally wise to assume that the necessary respect, prestige, and confidence to warrant acceptance as a leader must be earned. Such acceptance results from a consistent application of high personal standards and sound principles and from a good quality of decisions and ideas.

Subordinates should be well "serviced." They are entitled to coaching and training from their superior. He should see that their pay is right. Periodically he should let them know where they stand with him and the company. He should seek their advice on problems and keep them posted on new policies and programs. He should help them start new projects and carefully evaluate results of completed work.

He should outline their duties and responsibilities, preferably in writing, in terms which the subordinates can understand and so they have some leeway to move around. He should know his men and not burn himself out trying to change them too much—rather, he should be willing to adapt the job somewhat to the man.

Planning the work and having a program are great

assets in effective leadership. Too many executives are too busy answering alarms and putting out fires. This leaves inadequate time for the primary task of studying the causes of fires and planning for their prevention. The amount of time that can be profitably spent on planning probably varies from around 10 per cent for first level supervisors to 75 per cent or more at the top executive level.

Effective forward planning results in programs for achieving stated objectives or goals and includes alternate courses of action when unforeseen conditions arise. People turn instinctively to the man with a program, especially one of long range. Well worked out objectives and goals invariably result in improved organization coördination and increased over-all effectiveness. Many individual jobs as well as businesses as a whole have great need for better forward planning. This need provides interesting opportunities for growing business executives.

A leader should learn to inspire confidence and develop enthusiasm in subordinates. He should be a good listener, show a sympathetic understanding, and try to see the other fellow's viewpoint. He should keep the group "looking ahead" with a well worked out program. He should take an optimistic view whenever it is at all feasible and make subordinates comfortable when the "going is tough." He should show confidence by expecting much and letting subordinates know that he does expect much. He should compliment people when it can be done appropriately and sincerely, and he should look for opportunities to do so.

In working with subordinates it should not be forgotten

that one of the greatest human desires is to create or produce something, and to feel essential. And the constant trend toward narrowing or more specialized jobs and broadened or better informed people certainly adds to our growing human relations problem.

In considering this over-all area of working with people we should not ignore such easy sources of information as Dale Carnegie's *How to Win Friends and Influence People.* It might provide some useful pragmatic aids. Moreover, reading it is important on a simple defensive basis, because the chances are good that your superior, your subordinates, and your associates will have read it and are being influenced by it.

In a recent study by the United States Naval Institute of fifty-three leading companies, entitled "Personal Administration at the Executive Level," the conclusion was reached that more than 50 per cent of a top executive's time is spent on personnel management and that an important part of every supervisor's responsibility is personnel management. From my own observation during the past twenty years, that is the area which has presented the greatest hurdle to many men in developing business leadership. And that is an area requiring major attention in the future.

### MAKING DECISIONS

Sound business decisions are generally based on a combination of background knowledge, available facts, and exercise of judgment.

The knowledge element in decision-making is primarily derived from theories, principles, and practical experience.

The alert executive should, of course, learn to coördinate, group, and use other people's knowledge for their mutual benefit. This is particularly important from an experience standpoint, since it takes too long for one person to accumulate enough experience by himself to equip him for effective business leadership.

The facts element is highly important in arriving at correct decisions. It minimizes the great tendency toward emotional and prejudiced decisions. The ability to recognize facts, to know what facts are available in connection with each particular problem, to be able to assemble them, and then to analyze and interpret them, is fundamental to business leadership.

The judgment element includes drawing sound conclusions based on knowledge and facts. It involves (1) thinking effectively — sifting the important elements of the problem from the superficial; and (2) exercising perspective — seeing one forest rather than a large number of individual trees or vice versa, depending on what a sound solution of the specific problem requires.

The exercise of judgment in arriving at business decisions also involves being right much more than half the time. On the other hand, successful business leadership can be accomplished on the average by considerably less than a 100 per cent record in decision-making. A reasonable number of decision errors is part of the price of a progressive program.

### DEVELOPING AND SELLING IDEAS

A leader must get ideas easily. Hence he should try to develop his imagination. Ideas must first be obtained, then tested and timed for presentation, and finally sold to others for application.

Ideas usually originate from knowledge or research. Knowledge about the company can be obtained from reports and contact with others; about the specific industry from trade papers and associations; and about business generally from various literature and professional organizations. Research is, of course, a more formal source of ideas.

I believe that every important department in a business should continually apportion some of its time to research for new solutions and new ideas. Most businesses could probably justify more expenditures for formal research programs in five principal areas: product research, market study, industrial engineering, human relations, and forward-planning policies.

It is usually good technique to submit well thought out ideas without being requested to do so. They should be tested for their practical value and their presentation timed in the light of existing conditions. One's prestige is enhanced by having recommendations accepted. On the other hand, it must be remembered that prestige is weakened by having too many half-baked ideas turned down.

A leader must learn to sell ideas — to get his thinking across to others. One approach is to learn to write well organized, clear, convincing, and short memorandums. Another is to learn to conduct himself well in a conference, to go to a conference with a plan of attack, with suggestions, and not just to sit-in. And still another is to learn to speak to small and large groups; this not only builds personal prestige but is virtually a "must" for present and future business leaders. Effective leadership of a department, division, or company often involves direct talks to employees to supplement the line organization, to speed up policy changes, or simply to keep the internal channels of "up and down" communication well oiled.

One should feel and express conviction in selling ideas. The old saying, "be sure you're right—then go ahead," certainly applies. At the same time, the practical rules of working with people should not be ignored. To avoid creating negative resistance the degree of aggressiveness must be moderated by the proper amount of tact, finesse, and understanding. Business leaders must learn to effect a nice balance between "strength of conviction" and "dilution for diplomacy" under many varied circumstances.

### APPLYING THE LEADERSHIP FACTORS

These four areas, "Personality and character traits," "Working with people," "Making decisions," and "Developing and selling ideas" are not intended to include all the elements in effective business leadership. However, it seems to me that under present conditions these are the principal factors controlling the effective development of executive leadership—except for those somewhat nebulous and evasive elements of luck, coincidence, and opportunity.

It is well to assume that the elements of luck and coincidence are always present in varying degrees. It is necessary to be in a continuous state of readiness to meet them. Alternate defensive plans should be ready when the "breaks" are unfavorable and a forward program geared for action when they are favorable.

A leader should, and can, make at least a part of his own opportunity. His course should be charted in large measure in terms of his personal interests, traits, and abilities. The general tendency is to overvalue or oversimplify the other fellow's opportunity and to underestimate or unduly complicate our own; this is indeed a wasteful and misleading pastime.

A study of this type would be inadequate without a definite effort to determine what constitutes an effective mix of these abilities in individuals. Also there should be a realistic approach to the constantly shifting demands on executives as well as the need for the executive to shift his own motivating forces.

1. *The mix:* Not enough is known regarding the mix of leadership abilities which will produce the best result. Nevertheless, it probably can be said that a balanced development of most of the qualities and skills already outlined, without outstanding achievement in any one of them, will usually produce fair executive leadership. Also, my observation indicates that outstanding or better than average development in one area, plus at least average development in all other areas, usually produces superior results under conditions requiring the specific outstanding ability.

On the other hand, outstanding achievement in one area, with a decided weakness in another, and average in the remainder, often produces discouraging results. This type of unbalanced development usually results in executive failures, misfits, and frustrated climbers. The individual solution is to know yourself better and then change if possible, or at least supplement weaknesses.

If self-analysis indicates that adequate changes are unlikely, it would seem wise to revise personal objectives. The growing fields of vocational guidance and psychological testing should offer some assistance in solving such a problem. Also, budding executives certainly have a right to look to their superiors for intelligent guidance and personal coaching.

2. *Shifting demands:* The constantly shifting demands on executives require either nimble adaptation or a new type of executives for continued effective leadership of business enterprises.

I have in mind the increasing tempo of our social evolution. This requires improved human relations techniques and increased knowledge of the social sciences in contrast to the greater emphasis on mechanical techniques and the natural sciences in the past. The business leader must develop different concepts of labor and government.

Other examples of shifting demands on executives are the management evolution from ownership to professional-type management. Another is the current shift from production emphasis in time of war and early postwar to sales emphasis in a period of likely severe competition.

To cope effectively with these shifting demands, the successful business leader must have a keen sense of timing and adaptation. He must learn to "roll with the punch" and yet maintain a gyroscopic guidance for the business, keeping it within the confines of fundamental principles and headed toward a sound objective.

3. *Changing motives:* To be most effective a leader should also be happy and inspired. To maintain these attitudes under present conditions is perhaps more difficult

and serious than appears on the surface. The weakened monetary incentive resulting from high income taxes necessitates a drastic search for effective alternate motivations.

To supplement this weakened monetary incentive, we might consider improved offices, enlarged insurance and retirement programs, more lenient consideration of business club dues, greater vacation leeway, and perhaps increased allowances of other types. In short, build up the attractiveness of the job.

The strong ownership incentive could be brought back, somewhat at least, by governmental action to permit a practical and proper use of stock options for partial executive compensation. And greater freedom of time for more collateral activities, such as community and governmental affairs, could provide greater personal satisfaction for the executive.

All of us have a strong desire to contribute something to society. As Abraham Lincoln once said, "A man cannot be truly happy unless he is doing something for someone else." Community and governmental activities provide a vehicle for such happiness.

Moreover, successful business leadership in our currently evolving social structure requires that a larger proportion of time and energy be spent in these fields. Executives should see that our schools and churches know more about business, particularly its economic and social contributions and the real tie-in of business with the community. Our great industrial system, which has given us economic strength and a standard of living the like of which the world has never before experienced, is nevertheless on trial. If this system is to continue to evolve and grow on a sound basis that will be beneficial to all, then business leaders must accept new responsibilities.

Dean Donald K. David of the Graduate School of Business Administration stated it well in his recent report to the President of Harvard University:

> Mere technical competence in the affairs of business and in administration is not enough to qualify a businessman for either success or leadership. No man can be really competent in the operation of a business — in doing his part in the production of goods and services — without giving thought to the effect upon his own business not only of the rules and regulations imposed by society but also of its current hopes and aspirations.

These broadened responsibilities of today's leaders certainly require ***personality and character traits*** of the highest order, ***making decisions*** of great social significance, ***working with people*** on fundamental ways of life, and ***developing and selling ideas*** to keep our great industrial system functioning to produce the greatest good for the greatest number. Let us not forget that American business leaders are guardians of the only free economic system left in the world. Not only should we keep it sound economically but also see that it evolves in line with the hopes and aspirations of the people it serves.